How to Build

Fences
and
Gates

A Sunset Book

LANE BOOK COMPANY MENLO PARK, CALIFORNIA

Second Edition

Seventh Printing December 1964

LIBRARY OF CONGRESS CARD NO. 58-9946

TITLE NO. 110

Copyright © 1951, 1958

LANE BOOK COMPANY, MENLO PARK, CALIFORNIA

By the publishers of *Sunset* Books and *Sunset,* The Magazine of Western Living

LITHOGRAPHED IN U. S. A.

CONTENTS

YOUR FENCE . . . what will it do for you? 4

DRESSED PICKETS . . . neat and traditional 9

SLAT . . . lightweight, formal, versatile 13

RUSTIC PICKETS . . . grapestakes and woven saplings 17

BOARD . . . good design prevents boxed-in effect 24

SOLID PANELS . . . plant display and selective privacy . . . 31

LOUVER . . . tempered wind and sun 34

BOARD-AND-BOARD . . . attractive shadow play 40

BASKET WEAVE . . . economical enclosure 42

LATTICE . . . plant support or view frame 44

RAIL . . . the pioneers' fence 46

PLASTICS . . . soft light and silhouettes 53

GLASS . . . view without wind 58

WIRE . . . highly practical and lasting 62

COUNTRY FENCES . . . by the acre 66

CORRALS . . . horses' well being comes first 69

POOL ENCLOSURES . . . where security matters 71

HORIZONTAL FENCING . . . for hillside privacy 75

GATES . . . build for wear and abuse 76

FENCES AND PLANTS . . . mutual admiration society 86

FENCE DECORATION . . . color, design, lighting 89

WIND TESTS . . . which fence is best? 91

WHO BUILDS IT? . . . you, your neighbor, a contractor? . . . 93

FENCE LAYOUT . . . planning avoids problems 94

BUILDING MATERIALS . . . quality affects lifespan 96

PRESERVATIVES . . . protect posts against decay 99

POST HOLES . . . how to stake out, dig 102

ERECTING THE FENCE . . . how to go about it 104

CARE AND REPAIR . . . a springtime chore 110

FENCE LAWS . . . stay on the safe side 111

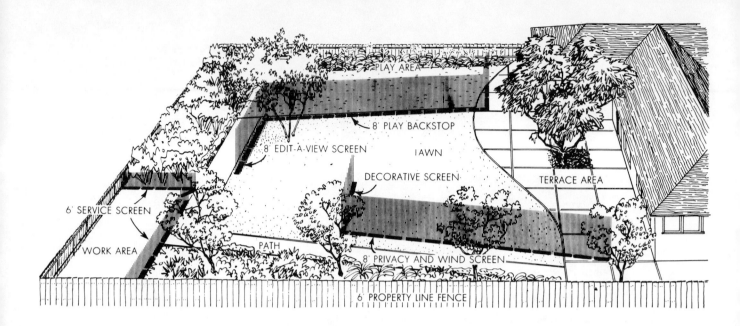

PLAY AREA

8' PLAY BACKSTOP

8' EDIT-A-VIEW SCREEN   LAWN

DECORATIVE SCREEN

TERRACE AREA

6' SERVICE SCREEN

WORK AREA   PATH   8' PRIVACY AND WIND SCREEN

6' PROPERTY LINE FENCE

YOUR FENCE... what will it do for you?

There is probably no homeowner more fence-conscious than the man who has moved into a new subdivision home, and who, as he looks out of his picture windows, sees his neighbors staring at him out of theirs. His first impulse is to rush out and put up a tall screen around his property to restore the privacy that his glass walls do not provide.

Once the fence is up he makes another discovery—he's got the privacy he wanted, but along with it there's a rigid, confined, boarded-up feeling that pens him in and lets him sense other pens around him.

Now, there's nothing wrong with putting up a boundary fence, but from the example above you can see that privacy is just one of several factors to consider when planning your fence program.

Traditionally most people think of a fence as a device that separates two pieces of ground, either physically, visually, or both. Many of the older fences we see were erected just for the sake of saying: "This is where your land ends and my land begins."

But as we begin to live outdoors more, and the garden becomes a visual part of the house, our whole concept of fencing changes. The fence can no longer be treated as a thing apart. Instead it is an *essential* vertical element in the landscaping plan, just as trees and vines are. And when used with a glass-walled house, the fence becomes part of the architectural scheme as well.

Our move into the garden creates a need for specific areas for work, play, and storage. Indoors we use walls or partitions to divide up the house; outdoors we use fences and screens to divide and add new dimension to the yard.

To develop your complete lot as living space, you also have to solve wind and sun control problems. You

can use fences to protect delicate plants, or create sheltered pockets to catch the sun or keep out prevailing winds.

When a fence functions as the wall of an outdoor room it can be decorated like an interior wall. Form, color, and line play an increasingly important part in fence construction. Decorative panels, designs, and complementary planting are some of the devices you can consider.

Naturally not every fence you erect will perform all the roles we've talked about above. However, if you keep in mind the possibilities in modern fencing, you'll be able to make your fences work at maximum efficiency. Let's take a closer look at some of the considerations.

SECURITY

The oldest service of the fence has been that of protection—to keep animals or people out or in—and it still serves that purpose today. Security today, however, is measured in terms of toddlers and small animals, not in terms of Indian attacks and elephants. No legal residential fence will deter an active 12-year-old boy. Naturally tall fences offer greater protection than the low variety. An open fence such as post-and-rail, louver, and board-and-board will admit small animals. If the fence is raised above the ground it will pass your neighbor's weed seeds and the snails escaping from his baits.

For ultimate security, metal chain link is best, though not the most attractive possibility. Appearance, however, is secondary to keeping small children off a busy thoroughfare or out of a swimming pool. Zoning laws in many cities require metal chain link fences or masonry walls when property borders a railroad track or freeway.

PRIVACY

Most people, when they think of fencing, think of privacy first. One way to get privacy is to rim the property with a high fence. The trouble is that this gives isolation instead of separation.

Acceptance of fencing varies from one area to another. In California, for instance, the basic fence is a 6-footer along the property line. In other parts of the country, however, a 6-foot fence is usually regarded as a curiosity or just downright unfriendly. But anything less than 6 feet high lets your neighbors see right into your yard —and house, when it has a glass wall.

You can sidestep the high boundary fence by screening for selective privacy. Put up short solid sections of fence where you need to interrupt your neighbor's line of sight; then open up the rest of your property line using rails, wire, or plastic. Sometimes, three or four neighbors get together and plan their yards as parts of one large garden. Boundaries are marked with inconspicuous wire fences to keep children and pets at home; the living areas are screened with baffle fences to provide privacy for each family.

In places where you *have* to erect a solid screen, do your best to make it handsome—from both sides. The fence won't seem as forbidding to your neighbor, who, after all, has to look at it too. The degree of privacy depends upon the type of fence you choose. *Maximum* screening is obtained with solid panels, close set grapestakes, or boards; *partial* by plastic, vertical louver, slat, and wire with vines; *least* with glass, lattice, bare wire, and post-and-rail.

WEATHER CONTROL

A properly designed fence can help you shape your garden climate by controlling sun and wind.

To control sunlight you can reduce glare with plastic panels or glare-reducing glass. Used in place of a solid fence, the plastics turn dark corners into softly lighted areas. For dappled shade, filter the sunlight through a louvered, slat, or basket weave fence. A vertical sun

screen around a patio will keep out the late afternoon sun that slants in under trees and roof overhangs. Such a screen will also cool the western wall of a house, stopping the hot sun before it reaches walls or windows.

You have two choices for controlling wind. If you want to shut off the wind, but preserve the view, use panels of clear glass. To break up a strong wind that spoils outdoor living, use a wind screen made of closely spaced slats, or one with a slanting baffle on the top. (See chapter on wind tests.) Remember that if you have a 6-foot boundary fence that doesn't stop the wind, you can sometimes erect a higher fence inside your lot for more protection. Check local regulations on fencing before you build any fence.

Be sure you know how the winds act in your yard before you put up a wind fence. Just because the prevailing winds come from the northwest in your area is no sign it will hit your garden from that direction. Sometimes a house will act as a giant baffle, and will roll a strong wind into the fence from behind, toppling it over. You can chart garden wind currents by hanging small flags about the yard and noting their movements when the wind acts up.

CREATING OUTDOOR ROOMS

Strategically placed interior lot fences work well as walls of outdoor rooms. One way to accomplish this is to enclose two sides of a patio that extends out from the living room. Or in an older home with a deep setback from the street, you can use screens and panels to reclaim outdoor living from the front yard. Furnish the resulting outdoor room to conform with your interior decorating scheme, using plants and color accents on the fence panels for interest highlights.

You don't need to stick close to the house for your outdoor rooms. Short, freestanding fences set in the middle of the yard separate the activities of the service yard, gardening center, and outdoor living area, and give you more usable space for outdoor work and play.

Choosing fences for outdoor rooms, you can really let yourself go because you don't have to worry about the neighbors' opinions. For a service yard you might want an open fence that lets air through, or a panel of aluminum to reflect heat against the drying clothes. Translucent plastic, lath, or wire make good play yard boundaries because they let you keep track vaguely of the children's activities. The wood pile, dog run, parking apron, and other "collecting" areas are also good candidates for interior lot fences. Materials selected, however, should harmonize with the feeling and tone of the garden and house.

Adding outdoor rooms to your yard also changes the apparent size of your garden. You inject a pleasant note of mystery into your surroundings when your guests can't see all your property at a glance. A small lot surrounded by a 6-foot boundary fence seems larger and less confining if you add a panel between you and the back fence. A large yard, on the other hand, becomes more intimate and cozy if it's broken up by interior fencing.

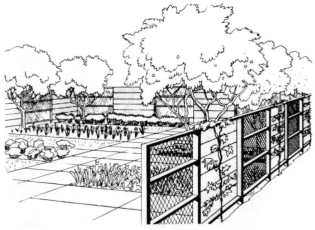

A 6-foot fence provides little wind control, but the high, 8 to 10-foot screen shown in corner makes a wind-free pocket

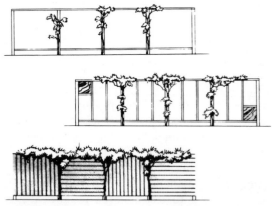

Here is a quiet terrace situated at the rear of a garden. The curved fence disguises the stiff, straight lines of the property

The pattern of this fence is varied by the use of alternating open and closed sections. An irregular pattern is more subtle

Fill in a basic fence frame with vines, wire, boards, or with any combination of these as you need them in garden design

Planning the walls of an outdoor room calls for an entirely different set of judgments than indoors. Outdoors, the trees, sky, your neighbor's roof, and the hills beyond are all part of your room, and you have to work with all of these elements at once. Often a fence will help screen out the objectionable elements in your landscape—a panel 4 feet wide may be enough to blot out a power pole or a neighbor's garage. Some vast uninterrupted views are too mural-like and static to be interesting. Even an open panel of wire mesh can make the view more stimulating.

There are no hard and fast rules for laying out fencing for outdoor rooms. Sometimes a single panel is enough for the illusion. The L-shaped fence works well in windy spots, while the T-shape and exploded T are very versatile. Whatever its shape, the fence should relate to the garden as a unit and not stand alone or as an afterthought. Keep it in scale with its surroundings,

and, if possible, keep it light looking. You get more continuity if you can repeat materials used in the house or a patio overhead.

FENCE PLANTING

Don't forget, as you work with your fences, that they can be changed more by planting than by construction. In many cases, plants, vines, and trees can do the same job as a fence. But plants take time to grow while a fence accomplishes the screening job immediately.

If you plan to use plants eventually as a boundary, you can use screens and temporary fencing as substitutes. One method uses temporary panels that can be removed and installed elsewhere when the plants mature. The fence posts are left in place, cut down to 3-foot height, and used for support wires or mesh screening.

A fence is a natural prop for plant material. Some

Short screens butting out from the side fence will provide secluded activity centers; good display panels for decorations

Partial fencing, or a free-standing screen, make small garden seem more spacious; serve as a trellis for climbing plants

Windows in the fence open either to neighbor's planting or distant view. Wire mesh keeps in pets and small children

By varying height of surrounding fences, you can prevent a small house from seeming to be engulfed by enclosures

plants that can't compete for attention out in the shrub border look very good against a fence panel.

Translucent plastic panels show off the structural

patterns of plants from either side of the fence. Even an open fence framework of two posts and a stringer seems to make a plant growing by it look more important.

Plants play an important part in dissolving the harsh lines of a boundary fence. One way is to plant so that portions of the fence disappear behind lush growth. Use vines and trees to break up the stern horizontal top line of a fence. There are also a number of espaliered plants that have been popularized by the increase in fencing. If you want a living fence, one that consists entirely of vines or shrubs, use wire fencing, lattice, or a trellis for support. One of the best features of a living fence is the cooling breeze that blows through the foliage, especially when it is wet.

Fences make good climate modifiers for plants. Plan for perennials on the sunny side, shade lovers like

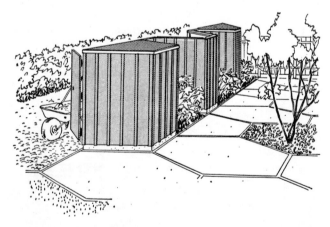

fuchsias on the other side. Citrus does well in some marginal coastal areas when set in a fence niche that traps the sun. In very windy locations plants need a windbreak to grow straight and bushy.

For frost protection you should design your fence with openings to let out cold air. Frigid air acts like water—it flows downhill and piles up behind obstacles.

A solid fence at a low point in the garden will dam up cold air with consequent plant damage. Leave a space between the bottom of the fence and the ground, or put in a gate that you can open during freezing weather.

BOUNDARY DEFINITION

There are points along the property line where screen fencing is out of place. If your nearest neighbor is a half mile away, you will need little, if any. In most sub-divisions, the front yard cannot be blocked in with a tall fence in the setback area.

A low fence, such as a post-and-rail or a picket, is often used around the front of the garden to identify your property line and protect your lawn and plantings. This is a particularly good idea on a corner lot where you need a traffic barrier to discourage short-cutters. On any lot, a low barrier will help keep bicycle riders, rubbish collectors, and deliverymen on your paved walks. Keep the bottom rail high enough to mow under unless you like working with lawn clippers.

A low boundary fence for its own sake, however, may look ineffectual, and just mean a high step for someone cutting across your property. Often it's better to claim as much of your front yard as possible for outdoor living with a high screen fence, and depend upon shrubs and plantings to control the traffic.

FENCE BUILDING

When you have made up your mind about the type of fence you want, you are ready to start building. Before you dig a single post hole, however, you should check with building officials about restrictions that may limit the height and locations of your fence. You should also be absolutely sure of your property line, even if it means having a survey run. Read the chapter on fence law at the back of this book.

If your fence is inside your property line, you can build it yourself; hire a contractor to dig the holes, set the posts, and leave the easy work for you; or you can assign the whole job to a contractor.

If the fence straddles a boundary line, you can do the job with a neighbor, pooling labor and dividing material costs; or the two of you can contract to have the hard work done by a contractor; or you can contract for the whole job.

Some people advise that it is simpler to erect a fence inside the property line, to avoid misunderstandings with the neighbors; but if you and your neighbors can agree on a fencing program you may all be better off.

For further information on fencing design and theory, see the companion *Sunset* book, *Landscaping for Western Living*.

Donald D. McMurray, Design; George D. Haight, Photo

Traditional colonial atmosphere of this early Monterey-style home is emphasized and enhanced by the dart picket fence painted white. Note how the pickets carry out the lines of the supporting posts and balustrade on second-story balcony

DRESSED PICKETS ... neat and traditional

A picket fence is an honest answer to the problem of separating your property from the public street or sidewalk.

It is a fence that is both reserved and hospitable in character. The militant line of pickets defines your property exactly and emphatically—no melting into the landscape for this fence. Yet, its low height and the openness of its structure invite the public to share the enjoyment of your front garden.

Traditionally, the picket fence has been associated with Colonial forms of architecture; but in actual use today, it is found paired off with almost any type of house. This is due to the inexhaustible range of picket designs and combinations that are available. There are literally hundreds of patterns for picket tops, ranging from squared ends that produce a simple, straightforward fence, to the intricate scroll-sawed patterns that make a formal design. Post caps range from plain flat tops to fancy ornamental shapes such as the acorn, pineapple, turned goblet.

In selecting an over-all design for a picket fence, you have four variables to work with: height of fence, width of picket, ornamentation, and picket

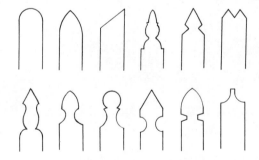

spacing. The typical picket fence is about 3 feet high, has 3-inch pickets pointed like the prow of a ship and spaced 3 inches apart. But all kinds of variations can be developed from these average qualities. Your fence may be 2 or 4 feet high, it may have narrow pickets widely spaced or broad pickets closely spaced, and the tops of the pickets may be rounded, square, or dart shaped.

Much of the effectiveness of picket fence design is due to its repetitive quality, but in a long stretch of fence, this becomes monotonous. There are various ways of introducing some variety into the pattern: use tapered pickets, slightly narrower at the top, to provide a subtle change; mix different width pickets together, alternating wide and narrow; or alternate pickets of different heights. For an inter-

minable length of fencing, such changes may not be enough, and you may have to alternate groups of pickets, as 3 broad, 3 narrow, etc.

DISADVANTAGES

Picket fencing· has some disadvantages. Some people feel that it is too commonplace and that there are fresher, more up-to-date fences from which

White picket fence is trim and friendly. Here the design of post heads illustrates one of many possible variations

Howard B. Hoffman, Photo

Picket fences go as well with the California ranch house illustrated here as they do with traditional colonial homes. The

brilliant colors of the climbing roses trained along the fence will emphasize the whiteness of the pickets in early summer

A close-up view of this fence shows a variation from the more pointed pickets usually used. This gives a softer look

to select. Picket fencing gives inadequate protection—it is an ineffective barrier to an intruder, children can clamber over it, and an agile dog can leap it or tunnel underneath. As most pickets are painted or whitewashed, they require periodic repainting, for they lose their crisp, neat appearance quickly if allowed to weather too long.

Pickets do not provide privacy and are thus inadequate for fencing an outdoor living area, unless it is also shielded by shrubs. This often compels the homeowner to install two types of fencing on his property.

CONSTRUCTION POINTERS

Picket fences are very easily assembled. Many lumber dealers carry all the necessary parts, already cut and ready to erect.

As a rule, it is better to buy the pieces in this manner than to attempt to cut the pickets yourself. You *can* do it, but you will need power equipment to help you cut and uniformly dress the vast quantity of pickets needed for a normal stretch of fencing. If you do decide to make your own, stay with standard-sized boards, such as 1 x 2, 1 x 3, or 1 x 4. For your picket tops, you can copy a pattern that you may have noticed on a fence or you can create

Max Tatch, Photo

Round-headed pickets used here. Lamp on corner post heightens interest. Hydrangeas peek through pickets

Miller & Warnecke, Design

Here wide spaces separate the oval-headed pickets. Divided gate is hospitably open. Right half of fence tops brick retaining wall

your own. Make a cardboard template. Use the cardboard the way children make valentine hearts: draw half the pattern, fold the cardboard, and cut out both sides simultaneously.

If you are planning to buy a prefabricated picket fence, make sure that it will fit your property. For instance, some varieties that are made up in finished panels cannot be used on a slope. The panels will not fit the posts.

If dogs and other small animals persist in digging under your fence, install a baseboard that runs a few inches below the soil. Use a 1 x 6 or 1 x 8 and impregnate it with preservative or it will rot away in a short time. You can also thwart them by nailing chicken wire to the bottom rail inside and burying it in the ground. It will not be noticed among plantings.

A molding strip, nailed on the outside of the fence parallel to the top rail, will keep pickets from working loose and deter small boys from removing a picket now and then.

If you select a picket with an unusual top design, you will be wise to order more than you need and keep a dozen or so stored away for replacements.

For protection against decay, picket fences should be back-painted. For details, see the construction chapters.

For variety white pickets set on low brick wall. An expensive and difficult fence, not recommended for amateur builder

Pickets set on top of wall of weathered stone make a good match for the trim, traditional-styled house. Note how the fence turns inward to outline the steps that lead up to the gate, emphasizing the entrance way and giving hospitable air

Eckbo, Royston & Williams, Design; Childress-Halberstadt, Photo

Long narrow slats of resawn, gray-stained redwood make dramatic background for interesting shadow pattern cast by Washington thorn tree. Silvery-leafed dusty miller beneath picks up the gray in fence. Plants and fence were considered as one complementary unit of form, texture, color

SLAT . . . lightweight, formal, versatile

Halfway between the picket fence and its rustic cousin the grapestake, is a type of fencing put together with long, narrow slats. Like the picket, it utilizes milled lumber, and like the grapestake, it is a tall, screen fence.

Material customarily used is rough-finished redwood, sawed into 1 x 1-inch or 1 x 2-inch strips. Since it is cut from standard lumber, it is not limited to the 6-foot height of the grapestake, and, where permissible, it can be used for higher fencing, as for a short, freestanding panel to serve as a planting backdrop or a strategically located screen.

Even though the strips have to be cut on order at the lumber yard, they cost about the same as grapestakes.

Slat fences are more formal than grapestakes, but they often look more truly at home in a city environment than their splintery relative. Their clean lines give a stronger vertical pattern than grapestakes with their irregular edges.

These fences are installed in two ways. They are nailed over a frame, like grapestakes, and set either snugly together or slightly apart. Or they can be overlaid on a solid fence to bring interest to an otherwise dull surface. Slats can be stained effectively.

Surprisingly, wind tunnel tests indicate that an open slat fence provides more effective wind protection than any other type of fence. The closely-spaced slats break up and disperse the wind. Fuller details about the tests will be found in another chapter.

John S. Bolles, Design;
Philip Fein, Photo

Vertical and horizontal combination of finished slats produces this striking screen fence of redwood. The 1 by 1's are set on diagonal, one inch apart. Upright supports are 4 by 4, with 1 by 6 cap

W. F. Severin, Design;
Childress-Halberstadt, Photo

Finished horizontal slats set in redwood frames, give a screenlike appearance. This is an imaginative solution to the problem of dividing a garden for family activities of widely diverse natures

Don Saxon Palmer, Design; Jerry Anson, Photo

An ingenious use of redwood slats to fence in the deck of a hillside home. Could be used equally well as a low fence surrounding a garden on level or hilly property. Vines in pots would train on slats

Eckbo, Royston & Williams, Design;
Tom Burns, Jr., Photo

Slat fences define garden, make good background for sculpture. All three utilize 1 by 2 materials which relate fences to one another; use of different heights and pattern avoids possible monotony

Lloyd Bond, Design; Tom Burns, Jr., Photo

Vertical slat fence curves around patio, makes excellent screen. Slats are redwood 1 by 2's nailed to 1 by 4 rails which are supple enough to bend easily. Rails are bolted between the double posts

Eckbo, Royston & Williams, Design;
Morley Baer, Photo

Thin boards are spaced close together at right for privacy from neighbors. When fence turns corner, where privacy is not consideration, spacing between slats is wider to let in light, save view

Calvin Straud, Design; George de Gennaro, Photo

The slat fence shown on the cover blends with the olive trees and eliminates view into the living room windows from front door. Slats filter light and wind

Eckbo, Royston & Williams, Design; Childress-Halberstadt, Photo

Honeysuckle grows informally on this screen of one- by one-inch redwood, hung from line of structural posts and enclosed with a one-by four-inch, weathered, gray-stained frame. Note shadow pattern

Osmundson & Staley, Design and Photo

Alternating slatted sections hide 2 by 4 stringers that support the fence. This design will be equally attractive from either side

George Jette, Design; Tom Burns, Jr., Photo

Above rock wall, cedar fence of 1 by 2 slats steps down slope, provides a handsome background for flowers

William Aplin, Photo

Along country roads in the Western United States split grape-stake fences have always been a common sight. Gray lichen, moss on the one pictured here attest to venerability of this construction. Now, grapestake is popular in residential areas

RUSTIC PICKETS . . . grapestakes and woven saplings

Drive down any road in the California redwood country and you will pass miles of irregular, picturesque fences made of moss-encrusted redwood stakes, driven into the ground.

Drive through any recent housing development and you are also likely to see miles of redwood stake fencing, for this is still a justly popular material for fence building.

This truly Western fence is built with the stakes that have been used in the vineyards for generations to support the grape vines. They are about 2 inches square, 3 to 6 feet in length. They are hand-split from redwood logs, hence have irregular edges. Stakes are usually split from heartwood, although sapwood varieties do find their way to market. If they are straight grained, knot-free, they can be re-split to make 1 x 2's. A better method is to saw them in half lengthwise on a bench saw. This produces a 1 x 2 with one rustic side for display, one smooth side for nailing.

Howard B. Hoffman, Photo

This grapestake fence with diagonal bracing fits into a natural background with ease. Just right for informal garden

Here, low rustic grapestake fence is fastened together with wire. This is an easy type of fence for the amateur builder

Grapestake fences owe their favor to several qualities. In the first place, they are decay-resistant and require no maintenance, except to drive home a loose nail now and then. The stakes are light in weight, easy to handle, and simple to install. The natural reddish tone that weathers to a soft gray blends smoothly with plantings, matches the warm tones of brick and stonework in the garden. Perhaps more than any other type of screen fence, grapestakes provide warmth to the barren lot when it is first fenced. Many types of fence merely accentuate the bleakness of an unplanted back yard, giving it an air of a prison quadrangle.

Grapestakes are adaptable to many different styles of construction. They may be driven into the soil; they may be nailed like pickets to a fence frame, pointed tip up for rustic effect, squared tip on top for a clean fence line; they may be fitted inside the frame to provide a two-sided fence; and they may be attached either vertically or horizontally, or in alternating panels of both to produce a change of pace in the fence design.

DISADVANTAGES

Grapestake fencing is often criticised. Many people feel that just too many miles of stakes have been erected in some localities, and that many in-

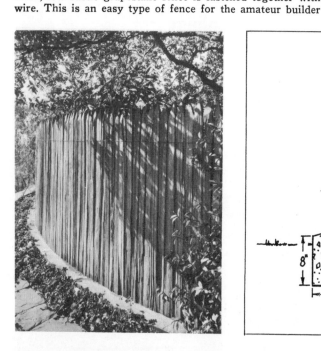

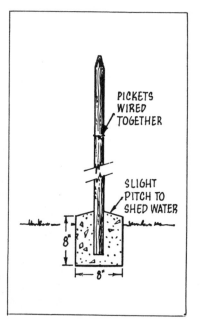

PICKETS WIRED TOGETHER

SLIGHT PITCH TO SHED WATER

8"

8"

This two-faced, gently curving grapestake fence offered quite a construction problem. The architect solved it by placing the stakes in a special concrete foundation

To keep stakes in desired alignment while the concrete is being poured and setting, wire the stake sections together ahead of time

When wired in 4-foot sections, the stakes can be lifted into place and secured into position by props or braces. Base of the fence is at a higher level than the garden

stallations have been made indiscriminately, without regard for the suitability of the fence to the house and garden. Some object to its splintery qualities, a hazard to pets and children. Some do not find pleasing the weathered gray to which it turns, considering it dirty looking.

Grapestakes are not cheap, despite their rough appearance. The fact that they are used in enormous quantities in agriculture tends to keep the price up.

CONSTRUCTION POINTERS

To save expense, split the stakes and nail them a short distance apart on the rail.

Wear heavy gloves when handling, as redwood splinters are ornery.

William Howson, Design; Ernest Braun, Photo

Staggered fence of grapestakes inside a 2 by 6-inch frame gives yard adequate privacy without completely enclosing it

William Aplin, Photo

This newly planted corner is warmed by a grapestake fence of weathered and uneven pickets which maintain informal note

C. Jacques Hahn, Design; Jerry Anson, Photo

Versatile grapestakes here enclose a patio of succulents with charming effect. Color variations in wood add variety

Handsome variation of rustic picket fence makes use of rosy bricks in low wall and posts spaced about 6 or 7 feet apart

Grapestakes stained white make a fence neater and more formal than unfinished lumber. Green vines provide contrast

Cedar grapestake fence supports streetside plantings. Three-foot height keeps out animals, but doesn't look forbidding

Here a low, even-topped grapestake fence encircles a patio of redwood squares. Note end of fence rolls back on itself

Grapestake with the bark still on the outside is both unusual and attractive. It is not advised for use near small children because of splinters

Problem of blanking out garage from sight of a view window solved with unpeeled grapestake

Lockwood De Forest, Design; William Aplin, Photo

The characteristic jointed appearance of bamboo provides an unusual background for the small fish pond in this garden

Howard B. Hoffman, Photo

The color and texture of these bamboo stakes with a rounded cap makes a pleasing background for the low flowering shrubs

Theodore Osmundson, Jr., Photo

Owners harvested crop of bamboo-like grass, Arundo Donax, created light patio windscreen

Osmundson-Staley, Design and Photo

Grapestake, usually considered informal, here is transformed into a fence of restrained dignity by the simple addition of a level cap on top

Henry Van Siegman, Design; John Robinson, Photo

Another example of formal type of grapestake. This one includes an open grill on the top; raised bed in foreground

Thomas Church, Design; John Robinson, Photo

Capped grapestake here is used in combination with a low brick wall. Planting between bricks and fence adds depth

Chandler Fairbank, Design

Above: Stepped-up grapestake fence along a driveway gives privacy; provides showy background for annuals and vines

Arthur Erfeldt, Design; Ernest Braun, Photo

Right: Free-standing fence used to screen small service area from main garden. Jog breaks up the line, gives stability

Morley Baer, Photo

Louver-type horizontal grapestake set on low brick wall assures privacy and keeps this patio cool on hottest days

Philip Fein, Photo

Here interlapping horizontal grapestakes act as a foil for the tall evergreens establishing a pleasant sense of balance

WOVEN PICKETS

Attractive varieties of rustic picket fencing are obtainable in prefabricated form, either made up in panels or woven together in rolls.

Woven pickets are easily erected, make an effective windscreen, and look equally well with their rough texture left exposed or when partly covered with vines. They are extremely durable and weather attractively.

This fencing is available in several styles: peeled, machine finished, or complete with bark; round or half-round; wired together or strung on steel rods. Wood is usually cedar, the variety depending upon the local species. Manufacturers in the Midwest and Northwest produce the largest part of these fences, and prices increase in proportion to the distance from the factory. If you order direct from the manufacturer, you may get a discount that approximates the shipping costs.

Above right: Peeled, split, half-round cedar saplings make an effective windscreen. Unpainted, the saplings weather nicely

Osmundson-Staley, Design; Philip Fein, Photo

Center: Cedar picket windbreak is placed on top of brick barbecue wall. These two materials are good color contrast

Ernest Wertheim, Design; John Robinson, Photo

Below right: Rounded, combed cedar stakes make good background for climbing vines; Gelsemium sempervirens used here

Douglas Baylis, Design; John Robinson, Photo

Below: Pickets wired together make this garden corner secluded. Vines could eventually trace pattern on the stakes

Successful solution to problem of how to make inside of fence attractive. Posts set between 2- by 6-inch rails used as base and top cap. Horizontal bats create shadows

BOARD . . . good design prevents boxed-in effect

The high board fence is a useful and easily-built type of fence, but one that demands skillful designing or placement to prevent its giving a cheerless, boxed-in feeling to the garden.

Its peculiarities force thoughtful design. It is an expensive fence because it requires a large amount of lumber, and consequently should justify its cost. In its solid form, it does give absolute privacy, but often at the expense of making a person feel imprisoned behind it. Its blank surface is monotonous and cheerless, especially in a raw garden, and offers a bleak vista from the house windows. In many of its forms, it has a definite right-side and wrong-side —which neighbor will get the framing to look at? If placed across the front of the property, it is likely to look inhospitable.

These sound like formidable hurdles for the fence designer to surmount. In fact, many homeowners have been discouraged by them and have settled for types of fencing that are friendlier and cheaper. But many others have approached the problem forthrightly and have designed and built solid board fences that are decorative and attractive. For that

To open up fence, boards are left off the supporting framework where there is no direct view into neighbor's yard

(24)

matter, many prefabricated fences are available that have grace and solidity.

PRINCIPLES OF DESIGN

Board fences can be given interest and pattern by a number of methods.

At a sacrifice of some privacy, a tall board fence may be opened up slightly to give a lighter feeling and a hint of the world outside. Boards may be set slightly separated like pickets, or they may be placed slantwise within the frame to form a louvered fence (discussed in a separate chapter). The upper quarter of the fence may be left open or fitted with an inset of lattice or open-spaced slats.

The blank surface area can be broken up by using materials that give pattern or texture to the structure, such as board and batten, siding, or tongue and groove; or by alternating panels with vertical and horizontal boards; or by varying the direction of the fence, using a zigzag or serrated fence line.

Horizontal siding will give the fence a strong horizontal feeling and appear to stretch a small garden; vertical siding will seem to compress a long fence.

The right-side wrong-side problem can be solved by designing the frame side so it has strong interest in itself, or by fitting the boards wholly within the frame so the fence appears the same from both sides. The frame side can also be improved with a simple trellis that will fill in with colorful vines.

A solid fence can be treated as an integral part of the house plan. Designed as an extension of the house wall to enclose the outdoor living area, it gives a feeling of continuity to outdoor-indoor living within its enclosure. Viewed through a glass wall, it becomes an outer wall of the house itself. Inner surface is therefore finished in materials that harmonize with interior wall materials and color schemes. The public side of the fence is surfaced with the same materials as the house — siding, shakes, board and batten.

CONSTRUCTION POINTERS

Board fences are simple to construct. A sturdy post and rail frame is built, as described in the construction chapters, and the boards are attached like pickets.

Dimensions are fairly standardized. Favored heights are 5 feet 6 inches or 6 feet. Posts are 6x6's or 4x4's set 6 to 8 feet apart. Standard 2x4's serve as rails. For fences taller than 5 feet, a third rail is often recommended.

These fences do call for substantial foundations because they are heavy and subject to wind damage.

Boards used should be of good quality. For knotless surface, it is necessary to buy select grades of lumber. For crackless joints, use boards with interlocking edges, such as shiplap or tongue and groove, or cover the joints between boards with battens.

Lawrence Halprin, Design; Ernest Braun, Photo

A decorative grid added to the existing support elements of this board fence breaks up a monotonous expanse of lumber

Osmundson & Staley, Design; William L. Strietmann, Photo

Structure of this redwood fence is a straightforward answer to the question of how to handle frame side of a solid fence

Roy Rydell, Design

A translucent midriff of 1 by 3-foot plastic panels gives an airy quality to this fence, and a soft lighting for the plantings in front of it. The horizontal fence boards are of 1 by 6-inch V rustic siding

Osmundson & Staley, Design;
John Robinson, Photo

Board fence of horizontal siding, supported from the back, gives a long clean line to the barbecue corner. Plant box, made of same material, and planting, create a pleasant and eye-catching spot

Jack Laflin, Design;
William L. Strietmann, Photo

Redwood board fence with diagonal slanted end makes excellent plant background. It uses 4- by 4-inch posts and 2- by 4-inch capping. Lights fastened on posts used for night effects in garden

John Robinson, Photo

The trim appearance of this solid redwood fence is heightened by use of sturdy vertical posts backing the horizontal boards and the smooth, low bricks edging terrace

Kenneth Schmidt, Design
Mason Weymouth, Photo

Low portion of this solid board fence conceals service area in an interesting way. Alternating horizontal and vertical white painted sections good backing for plants

Alvin B. Harrison, Design; Chas. R. Pearson, Photo

Modules of this fence step down to follow contour of hill. Fence marks the boundary of the yard, but 1-inch spaces between boards afford view of woods. Rustic 1 by 6's blend in woodland scene

Above: A baffle of solid boards blocks out view of the play area. The structure is tied into house for added stability

Left: Painted board fence built on curve. Note how fence is stopped short of tree, leaving it partly inside, partly outside

Widely spaced horizontal boards allow air and sunlight to filter into outdoor dining area, do not interrupt the view

Boards and hand-split battens were used in both house and fence. By repeating the theme, landscape design gains unity

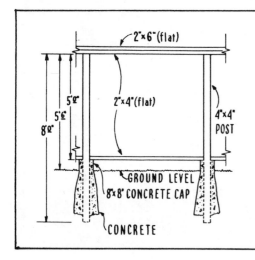

The choice of board fence designs is unlimited.

Above: Jog in line of redwood board fence provides pocket for plantings, relieves the plainness of the fence structure

Right: Board fence combined with overhead lath roof for plant shelter. Laths break early sun, fence shields in afternoon

Fence built with grooved siding placed vertically gives privacy to swimming pool, shields sunning bathers with tight surface

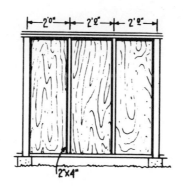

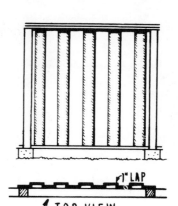

Here are ways of filling in a standard frame

∠ TOP VIEW

F. W. Bryant, Jr., Photo

Mason Weymouth, Photo

Board and batten fence becomes outer wall of open living room, matches interior color plan

Lower portion of this fence is shiplap siding, which matches the house and shows off the espaliered apple tree. Open post-and-rail tops the fence

Anshen & Allen, Design

When house is designed for maximum outdoor living, fence becomes one of its outer walls, and takes on its texture and materials

Sterling Leach, Design; William Aplin, Photo

Free-standing panels give immediate privacy, make simple background for plant display. Deodar cedar outlined against 4 by 8 panel of ¾-inch plywood, which is bolted to angle irons set in concrete to resist wind and clambering children

SOLID PANELS . . . plant display and selective privacy

Solid panel fence design offers some distinct advantages: Your fence goes up very quickly, particularly if your post module matches the panel size; you have a wide range of materials and textures from which to choose; the flat planes make good display surfaces; the panels insure complete privacy. On the negative side you should consider these drawbacks: the panels require strong structural support, especially in windy locations; a long panel fence seems confining; some of the materials need periodic painting to prevent weathering and warping. Here's a brief rundown on the panel materials:

Plywood is the old standby. It comes in a variety of species and thicknesses—most common size is 4 by 8 feet. For outdoor use you should specify the exterior grade. Because it has a tendency to warp and check, it should be painted regularly. It takes a high gloss finish. Seal the edges with white lead and oil, or by capping, and apply an over-all sealer to the surface before painting. Because of its weight and wind resistance its supporting frame should be substantial with well-set posts. A new plywood product which offers promise

Tito Patri, Design

A strategically located screen of hardboard blocks out an objectionable view of highway; sets off plants in foreground

Lawrence Halprin, Design; Ernest Braun, Photo

Gaily painted and decorated plywood panels brighten this outdoor living area, and keep it screened from street traffic

materials, hardboard needs stringer support between the fence posts to prevent it from bowing. For a play yard accessory, buy hardboard with a blackboard surface. Or you can get blackboard paint, which works on both hardboard and plywood surfaces.

Generally you'll have less waste if you work in standard panel sizes. Most of the panels in this chapter are available in 4 by 8-foot sections, which works smoothly into a 6-foot fence when cut as indicated below:

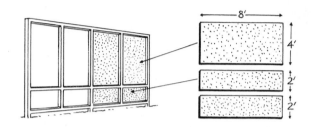

in fencing is Texture 111, an exterior, rough-finished plywood, grooved to look like individual boards.

Hardboard is made of wood fiber which is bonded under heat and pressure into 4 by 8 panels. Usually one side is smooth surfaced, the other screen textured. Preferred for outdoor use is the tempered variety, that is smooth on both sides. It comes in several textures— smooth, striated, corrugated, or perforated. You can paint it and expect good weather resistance. Allow for expansion and contraction at the joints. Like most panel

Asbestos board is the most durable outdoor material available. Made from cement and asbestos fibre, the panels are impervious to fire, weather, insects, and rodents. The panels take paint, and come in flat, corrugated, or striated form. Asbestos is heavy—a 4 by 8-foot sheet of ¼-inch material weighs 80 pounds, so you'll need heavy wood or steel posts to support it. Don't try to saw these panels—score them and break the same way you'd cut glass. Before erecting the panels, drill your fastening holes and attach with lag screws or bolts. The thinner sheets (⅛-inch) are quite flexible

Striated asbestos panels form back wall of this outdoor room. The 2 by 6-inch stringers make good display shelves

Osmundson-Staley, Design; Ron Partridge, Photo

Corrugated asbestos-cement panels fastened together zigzag fashion will support themselves with aid of light framework

and need support to prevent bowing. The corrugated variety, however, when erected in zig-zag fashion tends to support itself.

Corrugated aluminum provides a bright surface that is useful for reflecting warmth into dark corners of the garden. It's also good in a patio around a brazier or to reflect sunlight on clothes in a drying yard. The metallic sheen, often difficult to work into a garden design, can be painted over. Sheets are made in 26-inch width, and in lengths of 7, 8, 10, and 12 feet. The material doesn't rust, but it will corrode if allowed to touch the ground. It is soft and easily dented by errant baseballs or rambunctious children.

Corrugated iron has greater impact strength than the aluminum panels, and is better for children's areas. Though the panels are galvanized, they will eventually rust unless painted regularly. It is cheaper than aluminum.

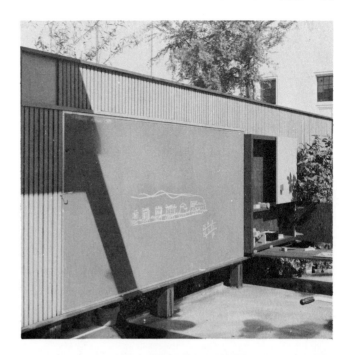

Osmundson & Staley, Design and Photo
Above right: Big 4 by 8-foot blackboard is ideal for the play area. It's made of specially surfaced variety of hardboard

George Meyer, Design; Tom Burns, Jr., Photo
Right: Galvanized screen of 4 by 8-foot panels hides service yard from outdoor living area. Posts are 4 by 4's; cap, 2 by 4

Donn Pierce, Design; Tom Burns, Jr., Photo
Below right: Painted panels of outdoor plywood set in open frame give deciduous trees a colorful all-year background

Barry Evans, Photo
Below: Folding aluminum screen, when placed around portable barbecue, reflects heat and keeps out cooling breezes

John Robinson, Photo

Lines of this vertical louver fence match architectural lines of house it surrounds. Note that vertical louvers do not keep out the glances of passersby from all angles. If privacy is main objective, horizontal louvers, as used in the gate, are needed

LOUVERS . . . tempered wind and sun

The louver fence is a handsome and useful type of fence but one that is quite expensive to construct.

Louvers give privacy without cutting off light and air or destroying the view. By adjusting the angle of the louvers, you can use the fence to con-trol several factors. By orienting them to the path of the sun, you can fix them so they furnish maxi-mum light and shade for plants. By facing them across the path of prevailing winds, you can temper the air circulation in your garden. And by setting them with their "blind" side toward the public, you can use them to screen a service area or a drying yard without shutting off the flow of air needed to disperse rubbish odors or speed the drying of washing.

Narrow panels can also be placed near entryways or front windows to permit the householder to view the street or entry walk but to prevent the passerby from observing the private doings of the family.

Vertically placed louvers provide only "progres-sive privacy," that is, some part of the garden is fully visible through the fence as a person moves along it. To secure absolute privacy, horizontal

Floyd Cowan, Design; John Robinson, Photo

Vertical louvered fence provides a patio for a master bedroom. Solid board at end assures the desired privacy from street

louvers are indicated. They will provide a more effective screen, but they are subject to structural weaknesses that discourage many builders from using them.

Louver fences are strong in design. The pattern of alternating strips of shadow and highlight, varying through the day as the sun's angle changes, provides an interesting feature in the garden. Louver fences are meant to be seen and consequently have to be carefully worked into the landscaping plan. They should not be concealed under vines or hidden behind shrubs. Over-planting along the fence line will close off the view and interfere with the free flow of air through the louvers.

Because of its architectural quality, louvered fencing should be matched to the design of the house itself. It is often treated as a part of the house, or as a means of tying to the house some element that is half-house half-outdoors, such as a car port or an outdoor room. If painted or stained the same color as the house, or a tone that complements it, this relationship can be further strengthened. Although it can be used with most styles of residential architecture, it appears least self conscious in company with modern-type structures that utilize simple planes, angles, and shadows to achieve their exterior lines.

DISADVANTAGES

Principal faults of the louver fence are its high construction costs and certain inborn weaknesses. The two are related, because much of the expense involved in erecting such a fence is due to the extra costs in premium lumber and careful workmanship needed to prevent the fence from deteriorating.

Several factors force the costs upward. In the first place, louver fencing requires a larger amount of material than any other wooden fence. More vertical boards are required per running foot than for a solid-board fence of comparable height. Secondly, the louvers are supported only at the ends without center bracing, and this tends to encourage them to warp and twist after several months' exposure to sun and rain. To prevent this, many fence builders use top-grade (and top-price) kiln-dried lumber, and apply some variety of moisture seal. If the louvers are installed horizontally, they are sure to develop a sag unless the span between the posts is fairly short or the boards are supported in the middle.

Another complication is due to the heavy weight of the fence structure. Much of the weight of the louvers is borne by the bottom rail, which may sag and throw the framing out of alignment. And

W. Leighton Clark, Design

Adjustable louvers close for weather protection; open when you desire to capture summer breeze and let in the view

Hallauer & Schmidt, Design; William Strietmann, Photo

The sun casts an attractive shadow on this redwood louver fence. Note contrast in color of cap with the fence material

the whole structure requires stanch posts and substantial foundations.

Finally, louver fences consume a surprising quantity of paint, because of the unusually large surface area that must be covered.

All of which explains why you rarely see louver fencing used for long, meandering boundary lines. It is usually found in fairly short installations, placed expertly where fullest advantage of its features can best be obtained.

CONSTRUCTION POINTERS

There are two ways of building a louver fence.

You can set the posts, attach the top and bottom rails, and nail the louvers in place, toenailing them to the bottom rail and driving through the top rail.

This is most easily done by two persons, one officiating at the top rail, the other working the lower one. If one person were to attempt this method, he would soon tire of popping up and down.

The other system is to construct the fence in sections on the ground, then lift the completed panels

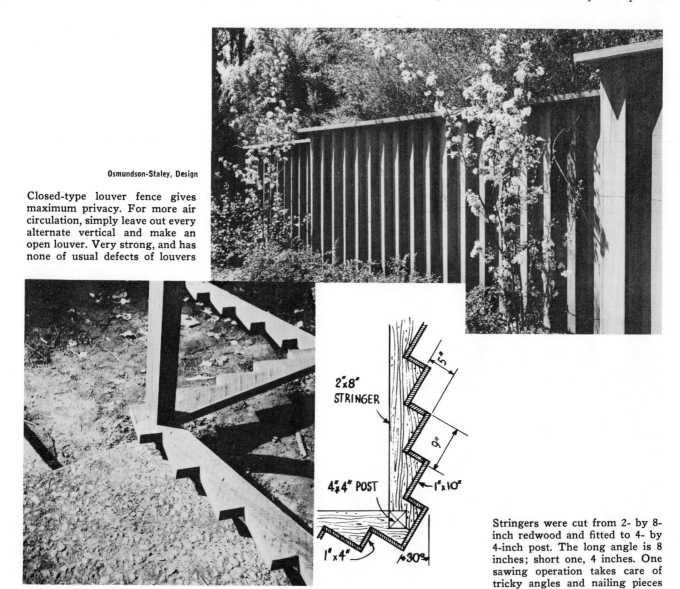

Osmundson-Staley, Design

Closed-type louver fence gives maximum privacy. For more air circulation, simply leave out every alternate vertical and make an open louver. Very strong, and has none of usual defects of louvers

2"x8" STRINGER

4"x4" POST

5"

9"

1"x10"

1"x4"

30°

Stringers were cut from 2- by 8-inch redwood and fitted to 4- by 4-inch post. The long angle is 8 inches; short one, 4 inches. One sawing operation takes care of tricky angles and nailing pieces

into place, and nail them to the posts. If you have a good flat surface on which to work, such as a driveway or garage floor, you may find this method the easier of the two.

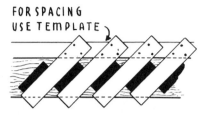

FOR SPACING
USE TEMPLATE

Louvers can be set at almost any angle, some are installed at right angles to the fence line, but the accepted angle is 45 degrees. To make sure that the louvers are spaced properly for nailing, use a template. With it, you will not have to measure for each board.

You should use boards heavy enough to resist warping—2x4's or 2x6's are good.

Attach a beveled or slanted cap along the top to shed rain water and keep it from seeping into the exposed grain of the wood.

You can sometimes reduce the cost of construction by eliminating posts and constructing the fence on concrete foundation pylons with nailing surfaces.

For a thoroughly rigid fence that looks like a louvre fence but has none of its structural weaknesses, build a closed-louver fence such as the one described below.

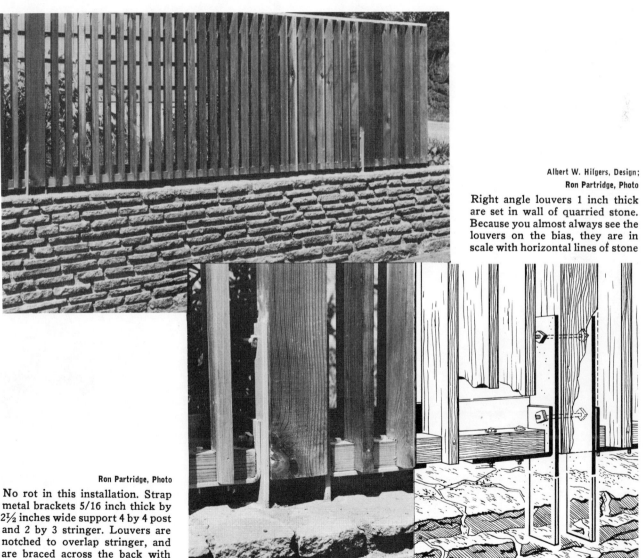

Albert W. Hilgers, Design;
Ron Partridge, Photo

Right angle louvers 1 inch thick are set in wall of quarried stone. Because you almost always see the louvers on the bias, they are in scale with horizontal lines of stone

Ron Partridge, Photo

No rot in this installation. Strap metal brackets 5/16 inch thick by 2½ inches wide support 4 by 4 post and 2 by 3 stringer. Louvers are notched to overlap stringer, and are braced across the back with 1 by 4 board that runs full length

Above: An attractive louver fence, but not too practical in construction. Unless built of kiln-dried lumber, wide-spanned louvers tend to warp and sag after exposure

Ernest Wertheim, Design; John Robinson, Photo

Left: Here louvered wall adds height to raised bed arrangement. Also, provides good air circulation for growing plants. Note how vine is making itself at home on sunny louvers

Jerry Anson, Photo

This fence was designed primarily to aid in protection from summer heat. The horizontal louvers with ample open space above provide the maximum possible air circulation, as well as affording the utmost in privacy for the shelter occupants

Philip Fein, Photo

Trim louver fence achieves dignity. If privacy is main object, be sure louvers are set at right angle to provide it. Note that you can see through the louvers at end of this fence but not the ones on the side

Angus McSweeney, Design;
Mason Weymouth, Photo

Fences may be used to cut out undesirable views. This one of alternate louvered baffles and open wire sections meeting at right angles was designed to give privacy from a well-traveled road

Morley Baer, Photo

Broad louvers complement lines of modern architecture to produce trim fence. Provide enclosure to outdoor-indoor without seeming to box it in. Allows air circulation

William Aplin, Photo

Variation on popular shadow or board-on-board fence is this vertical adaptation. This type is not as easy for small fry to climb over as the horizontal variety

BOARD-AND-BOARD . . . attractive shadow play

The so-called board-and-board or shadow fence, popular in Japan, offers possibilities to the home-owner who would like to secure the advantages of a louver fence without having to pay its heavy installation cost.

It is simply built. Boards are nailed to the frame with an open space slightly narrower than the board left between them. Another set is then nailed to the

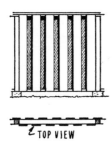

TOP VIEW

other side, with the open spaces opposite the boards on the first side. The fence is thus the same on both sides.

Robert Mosher, Design; Robert C. Cleveland, Photo

Another example of the vertical shadow fence, here shown enclosing sunken patio. Features privacy with ventilation

The baffle-like arrangement of the boards breaks up strong wind currents but allows air to circulate freely. Like louvers, when the boards are placed vertically, they give filtered privacy and light; when they are set horizontally, they give absolute privacy, but pass no direct sunlight. This fence also takes on interesting shadow patterns as the sun advances, in contrast to straight board fencing.

One great advantage: this fence can be assembled with mediocre lumber, because a small amount of warping is not noticeable with this design.

DISADVANTAGES

The fence is limited in value as a security fence. Small animals can wiggle their way through either vertical or horizontal panels, and the horizontal variety offers an attractive climbing surface for children and intruders.

CONSTRUCTION POINTERS

Although this is an exceptionally strong fence, it usually calls for extra bracing to prevent the boards from sagging. An extra rail, halfway between top and bottom, will keep the vertical boards from warping; an extra post or 2 x 4 at the 4-foot mark will keep horizontal boards from sagging.

Morley Baer, Photo

Horizontal board-on-board construction has pleasing appearance and gives absolute privacy, but no direct sun penetrates

Smith & Williams, Design; Julius Shulman, Photo

Here board-on-board construction in its horizontal form encloses charming patio. Note how vines climb between boards.

Boards do not touch each other in shadow construction, so may be made successfully from less expensive lumber grades

Douglas Baylis, Photo

Basketweave fence looks complicated, but once you master construction techniques, fence grows quickly and inexpensively. Note the shadow patterns which help to make this fence outstanding

BASKET WEAVE ... economical enclosure

Basket weave fencing uses a minimum of material to get a solid screen, is attractive from both sides, and surprisingly strong for its weight. It's a favorite with contractors because they can use inexpensive half-inch stock in construction. Some people, however, find the weave dizzying to view in large quantities, and everyone will agree it's a difficult fence to paint.

CONSTRUCTION POINTERS

1. For the strips, use almost anything you happen to have at hand. Rough-finished lumber is usually preferred because it gives softer texture. Strips should not be thinner than ½ inch, thicker than 1 inch. They can be 4 to 12 inches in width, but preference favors 6-inch. Strips can be any standard length, from 14 to 20 feet. Four by 4-inch posts should be spaced according to the length of the strips.

2. Nail strips only at posts, but don't start off every strip on a post. Alternate centers and ends.

3. Halfway between the posts, separate the strips with 1 x 1-inch spacers or 1-inch rounds.

Henry Van Siegman, Design

Plantings often help to soften dizzying effect of the basket weave pattern. Here espaliered pyracantha masks fence

4. As a rule, no rails are needed, although there are some designs that make use of them, as shown in the drawing.

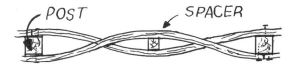

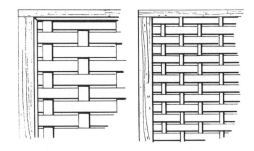

5. Paint the fence before assembling.

In one variation of basket weave, lightweight strips are criss-crossed in a tight weave. This type does not let air circulate so freely, and it is a mean project for an amateur to attempt. It is best woven on the ground and then attached *securely* to the frame.

John Robinson, Photo

Long wood strips of cigar box thickness are used in a diagonal pattern in this refined variation of the woven fence

W. L. Strietmann, Photo

For variation, here is a flatter type of basketweave fence. The spacers and horizontal strips are both made of redwood

Jerry Anson, Photo

Posts used as spacers achieve a very wide, open basketweave. Arrangement of sections provides interesting baffle gateway

Charles R. Pearson, Photo

Pots of brightly colored flowers are the accent note on this white painted lattice used for screening a work area

Thomas Church, Design; Morley Baer, Photo

Closely woven lattice imposed on wall is excellent background for an attractive climbing vine of graceful growth pattern

LATTICE . . . plant support or view frame

Lattice fences can be used for several purposes in the garden. A tightly woven lattice can be used to screen out an objectionable view, or shield a service yard or garden work center. With its spaces opened wide, a lattice will let in a view, serve as a traffic director, or double as a display tier for potted plants.

Lattices may be used to support climbing roses and other vines. However, such plantings must be kept pruned or they will run away with the fence. They also have to be removed to permit periodic repainting. As some vines damage wood by keeping it too damp; check with your nurseryman before planting alongside a lattice fence.

Lattice work can also be used to liven up the blankness of a solid wall. When attached to the wall, it should be fastened on so it can be removed or lowered at repainting time.

Only construction tip is not to build the lattice-work too light if it is to support plants. Don't underestimate the weight and drag of a matured vine.

Philip Fein, Photo

Wide lattice-type frame holds a variety of flower pots

Thomas Church & Associates, Design; John Robinson, Photo

Above: Lattice takes over separation duties when complete visual block is not needed. Grid squares are 9 by 9 inches

Osmundson & Staley, Design; Philip Fein, Photo

Above right: Wide lattice-type frame holds a variety of flower pots out of the way of damage from small-fry vehicles

Paul Thiry, Design; Art Hupy, Photo

Center: Handsome, lightweight lattice runs along one side of patio, screens outdoor area from walk approaching house

Jerry Anson, Photo

Below: Lattice of slender laths is being used as a base for training a pattern of vine. Construction detail is shown at left. In planting vines on this type of lattice, care should be taken that vines chosen will not grow too heavy for fence

William Aplin, Photo

Post-and-rail fences look at home on the ranch. Horizontal lines follow rolling country; sturdy construction confines stock

RAIL . . . the pioneers' fence

Today's rail fence is a direct hand-me-down from pioneer days.

Most venerable form is the picturesque zigzag variety seen occasionally on a country road. It was a by-product of the forest-clearing days, when wood was plentiful and a nuisance and when boundary lines were flexible enough to take a broad-gauge fence. When timber and land began to become more valuable, the kinks began to disappear from this type of fence and it straightened itself out. As timber became even more marketable, the fence began to shed rails, finally arriving at the two- and three-rail variety popular today.

Last step in the evolution was a shift from split rails to sawn lumber, from post-and-rail to post-and-board. This conversion was inevitable when dressed lumber became less of a novelty to the fence builder than raw timber.

The rail fence is ideally suited to the country scene. Its horizontal lines follow gracefully either rolling or flat terrain. It is economical in lumber usage, particularly if it is built of raw materials near at hand. A sturdy fence, it is effective for containing cattle, horses.

Some varieties fit easily into urban landscaping. Light rail fences go best with ranch style homes but look well with many other styles. One- or two-rail post-and-board or low split-rail fences make excellent definition fences for the front yard. They discourage pathfinding but don't block the view or shut off sunlight to plants.

As a type, rail fences are less expensive than picket or board fences. Some of them are the simplest of all fences to build, requiring only casual workmanship. The more sophisticated varieties, with fitted mortise and tenon joints, do call for more painstaking work.

(46)

RAIL FENCE EVOLUTION. Upper left: Pioneers built fences out of timber culled from clearing forests, didn't mind meandering property line. **Upper right:** Zigzag straightened out in this manner when wood became more valuable. **Lower left:** Fence shed unnecessary rails, lengthened distance·between the posts. **Lower right:** Dressed lumber succeeds split rails

ZIGZAG FENCE

If you have a surplus of timber on your country place or would like to create a rustic effect in your garden, you can put an old-time zigzag fence together with little trouble.

Use split rails or 2-year growth. Assemble fence by setting double posts beside the rails where they cross, or by splitting the ends of each rail and interlocking the splits, or by driving dowels or steel pins down through the rails. If you use heavy wood, weight of the rails will hold fence without additional support.

SPLIT RAIL

In this type, the rails are laid one on top of the other and held in line by posts set in pairs alongside the overlapping ends. It can be built with rails of any size and weight, but its most popular Western form is fashioned with grapestakes.

The horizontal grapestake is inexpensive, requires no upkeep, and is easy to build. It is found in various heights, ranging from a miniature fence two or three rails high for rimming a flower bed, to standard-height fences for enclosing a vegetable garden or an orchard. Its weaknesses: not a strong fence, it will not withstand climbing children; and it will not exclude some animals.

Construction is simple. Lay out fence line as described in construction chapters. Distance between posts should be a foot or so shorter than length of rails to allow for overlap at each end. Set paired posts in hole or drive into ground. Place them the width of a rail apart, using a piece of rail as a spacer gauge. Set all the posts before stacking the

Mason Weymouth, Photo

Above: Well-built, hand-split rail fence lasts practically forever with minimum of maintenance; uses excessive materials

Jack Gibson, Design; Philip Fein, Photo

Left: Modern version of zigzag fence, made of stained 2x6's, held together with ½-inch steel pins where rails interlock

Maynard Parker, Photo

Post-and-rail fence built with dressed posts, hand-split rails, duplicates textures of house with its blend of stone, dressed siding

W. P. Woodcock, Photo

Lightweight post-and-rail surrounds ranch style home. Note matching gate. Gate stop formed by extending top rail through the latch post. Fence, gate are white

Above: Whitewashed, split-rail fence is held together by strong wooden dowels which run through each rail and into the post

Right: Horizontal grapestake fence is inexpensive, requires no upkeep and is easy to build. Rails nailed or wired to posts

Charles R. Pearson, Photo

This low, decorative grapestake fence is used as a traffic barrier; unobtrusively keeps strangers and guests from cutting across lawn. Split stakes match house exterior

Philip Fein, Photo

Miniature redwood rail fence used to define boundary. While attractive, would be more practical if lower rail were high enough to clear wheel of the lawnmower

Above: Rail fencing gracefully follows the contours of the countryside. Whitewashed boards nailed to round, peeled posts

Left: Two examples of mortised posts. Note how the tops of posts have been shaped to shed rainwater, forestall decay

rails in line. Attach rails to posts with galvanized wire, twisted tight, or with nails driven through posts.

POST-AND-RAIL

The old-fashioned post-and-rail, a handsome and long-lasting variety, is still popular in many areas for enclosing stock pens, fields, or orchards or for giving a decorative border to a ranch type home layout.

The fence requires little maintenance because there are no spikes or wires to rust and work loose.

Posts are made from round peeled lengths of timber, 6 to 8 inches in diameter. They are usually set 2½ feet into the ground, so they provide stanch support for the rails. Mortises are cut all the way through them to hold the rails, which are tapered to wedge inside. Rails consist of long poles, cut from second- or third-year growths.

Posts are customarily placed 10 feet apart. This long span requires that the rails used must be strong enough to support their own weight without sagging.

Construction calls for some skill in handling tools. Rail ends are shaped with an axe or draw knife, mortises are bored out with a large auger and then smoothed with a chisel. It is rough work, for the posts and poles are quite heavy to handle.

If you want to avoid the carpentry phases of erecting a post-and-rail, you can buy the fence materials already shaped to fit. Well-made, natural-looking prefabricated post-and-rail fences are obtainable from dealers.

To set up this fence, dig the post holes, plant the first post; fit the rails into the mortises, and then set the next post in its hole. Fit the other ends of the rails into the second post, tamp it firmly in place; then wedge in the next set of rails, and continue in this sequence around the fence line.

POST-AND-BOARD

The post-and-board fence is the direct descendant of the post-and-rail. It is substantially the same fence, but built with dressed lumber instead of hand-hewn timber.

The typical post-and-board fence is 3 to 4 feet high and has three rails. Two- and four-rail types are also common. Rails are set varying distances apart. If the fence is used to pen stock, rails are spaced closely enough to keep a horse or cow from poking its head through.

Posts are heavy-duty, either 6x6 and 8x8. They are sunk in the ground 2½ feet.

There are two main types of post-and-rail fencing. With one, the rails are let into mortises in the posts in imitation of the old-style post-and-rail. With the other, rails are nailed to the sides of the posts.

Mortised rails—Posts are mortised to take rail tenons (see construction chapters) in one of two ways: a broad mortise lets the rails overlap side by side; a long narrow one lets them overlap one above the other. When rails overlap at the side, a very wide and heavy post is needed, but this joint adjusts more easily to sharp changes in grade than a joint with one rail above the other.

Span between posts may be 8 to 12 feet, depending on the weight of the rail (2x4, 1x6, etc.). Posts may be solid or made of three or four layers of lighter wood.

Lapped joints—When the rails are attached to the sides of the posts, lighter weight boards are usually used for rails and the span between posts reduced to 8 feet. Favored weight boards are 1x6's or 1x8's.

The top rail is often attached with a slant. This makes the fence look sturdy, prevents children from walking along it, and protects the tops of the posts from rain. Rails so set, however, sag eventually.

Setting the top guard rail at an angle keeps children from walking fence, makes it stronger, and protects ends of posts

Batten on foreground post—missing on the others—improves appearance of fence, protects ends of boards from weathering

Unpainted bamboo and redwood make an inexpensive oriental type fence, good with leafy plants. Pickets last about two years

Jerry A. Anson, Photo

Two-rail post-and-board used to connect informal living center with more formal house. Note cap rail, protects top rail

Carol Eyerman, Photo

Lattice combined with post-and-rail gives airy, finished tone to fence and does not block view. Diamond bracing is strong

Howard B. Hoffman, Photo

Post-and-rail with lattice pattern looks trim and orderly when set on top of a red brick wall. Posts and rails are 2x2's

Children and pets escape through post-and-board fences. They can be confined by substituting slats for the middle rails

Philip Fein, Photo

Here is the post-and-rail reduced to its simplest components, yet adequate for defining a boundary, discouraging trespass

John Carmack, Design; Phil Palmer, Photo

Fence that encloses this outdoor room is made of plastic screen panels, which alternate with modules of bamboo. The plastic keeps out more wind than bamboo, provides restful lighting. Note the plant silhouettes against the screen

PLASTICS ... soft light and silhouettes

Sometimes the fence builder has to solve a problem of cutting out glare or blocking off a view without sacrificing any sunlight. Formerly the only solution was to install panels of obscure glass, but in recent years plastics — in screens, panels, and sheets — have taken over a large part of this job. It's probably safe to say that the next few years will see a number of new plastic materials in outdoor building roles once performed by traditional materials. Here's the way plastics stack up today.

PLASTIC SCREEN

This is the oldest of the proven plastic materials. It consists of regular window screen sealed in a sandwich of translucent plastic. It has several properties that recommend it to the fence builder. It diffuses sunlight to a soft radiance that looks cool as ice water in the garden. The silhouettes of plants behind the screen have the subtlety of a Japanese print.

It is quite useful for screening service areas—the eye can barely see the garbage can lurking behind the screen —or reducing the neighbors to a blur. Yet, it performs

Morley Baer, Photo

Dramatic night lighting behind translucent plastic panel breaks dark expanse of boards, shows off plants in silhouette

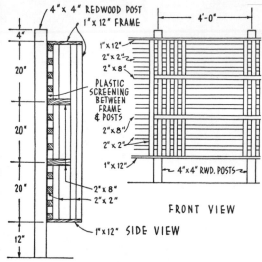

Eckbo, Royston & Williams, Design; William Aplin, Photo

Plastic screening backs up patterned grid, which is 3-dimensional for interesting shadow effects

this discreet service without cutting down the sunlight needed in a kitchen window or an outdoor room.

Perhaps the quality that endears it to the homeowner is that it is cheaper initially than the varieties of obscure glass or rigid plastic for which it substitutes. In the long pull, however, one of the former may prove to cost less per year, because the screen has to be replaced every few years. The plastic seal eventually gives way and the wire rusts.

Install the plastic in the same way as you would porch screen. Attach it with battens or molding strips so it can be removed easily when it is damaged or rusts. The fences shown on this page illustrate another good point—using a grid-like fence to reduce the size of each section of screen. The material isn't designed to take strong wind, which will stretch the wire and break the plastic seal. The grid structure keeps windstrain to a minimum and lengthens the life of the fence. One caution: don't use the screen in an overhead or wind baffle slanted off the top of a fence. It will deteriorate rapidly if water, dirt, or leaves are allowed to collect on its surface.

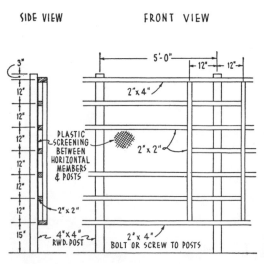

Eckbo, Royston & Williams, Design; William Aplin, Photo

With lightweight frame, plastic screen has good lateral support; note yard doesn't seem small

With these two portable screens, owners shift their outdoor arrangements to fit wind control and privacy requirements.

The screens are 8 feet long, mounted on casters to slide under roof overhang. Support frame is 2 by 2's and 1 by 2's

PLASTIC PANELS

These more rigid cousins to the plastic screen have much the same light diffusing qualities but they are less translucent. They have a longer life expectancy, but just how long isn't known for sure, since these materials are still relative newcomers to the fencing field.

Most of the panels have a fiberglass core sealed between layers of polyester resin. Several colors are available and some types have leaves, butterflies, and other elements imbedded in the plastic. Flat, corrugated, and textured styles are offered.

They are easy to install, can be sawed and nailed. Use a fine-toothed hand saw, or an abrasive disc on power tools. Otherwise the material tends to craze along the saw cut. A heavy hammer blow may break the bond between the fiberglass core and the resin, clouding the panel in that spot. Pre-drill holes and use aluminum nails and neoprene washers when fastening. Since the panels are quite flexible, you'll need to add extra support when they are used over long spans. They are lightweight and easy to handle, practically impervious to weather, though some of the colors tend to fade in long exposure to sunlight. Surface erosion may impair the light transmission. If you are using a concentrated garden spray near a plastic fence, check the specifications of both products. Concentrated sprays will eat through some

Plastic screen fence along sidewalk insures yard privacy, lets in light. Shrubs planted flush against fence for silhouettes

Corrugated rigid plastic panels work as windbreaks, baffles, planting screens. Material is tough, but it takes support about every 3 feet to prevent bowing. High wind resistance means that the panels should have firm anchor in the ground

Light reflected off the ocean makes this panel change color as the water does. Dark vertical lines show panel lap joints

Flat version of rigid plastic panels backs up an entry garden. Grid is decorative, but also provides much-needed support.

Sanford Hanscom, Design; Darrow M. Watt, Photo

Curved clear plastic screen of butyrate protects northwest patio from prevailing winds, but preserves view of orchard at the rear of property. This screen could act like a sail in a high wind, so set posts deep and batten plastic down tight

plastics. Normally, however, sprays in dilute form will not hurt polyester panels.

Some people object to the fading and the limited color selection. Others feel the material has a quality foreign to the garden atmosphere. Sheets come in various sizes, but standard width is 26 inches in lengths from 3 to 12 feet. It's expensive and the high cost causes many to use it sparingly, usually just as an occasional panel to lighten a solid fence, or to capture a particular lighting effect.

NEW PLASTICS

The butyrate wind screen shown on this page is a sample of the things to come in the plastic field. This plastic is semirigid, sold in a roll. It's economical cost per square foot makes large-scale use feasible. Although it appears to be one continuous wind screen in this installation, the plastic was actually cut into panels 42 inches wide, the width of the roll. The panels are set at angles to approximate a curve, but each panel is actually flat. Life expectancy of the butyrate is set at 5 years.

The more fragile films, such as polyethylene or vinyl, seldom last longer than a year in direct sunlight, which destroys them. Neither of the latter is suitable for any more than very temporary fencing purposes.

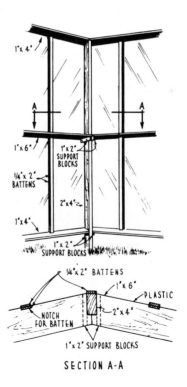

Double battens sandwich the plastic. Inner battens set in horizontals so plastic lies flat; outer bats nailed to 2 by 4's

Butler Sturtevant, Design;
Bob Lackenbach, Photo

Here a lattice frame was filled in
with glass panels. Later these
were changed to mirror panels to
increase apparent size of garden

GLASS . . . view without wind

There are many locations where the difference
between comfort and discomfort out-of-doors is
determined by the wind rather than temperatures.

When the air temperature is at a comfortable 70°,
a breeze of but eight miles per hour will cool you as
much as a temperature drop of 12°.

It's difficult to realize how much difference a
windbreak will make until you have built one; and
the increase in comfort is always matched by more
favorable gardening conditions.

Along some sections of the coast where summer
temperatures are never high, and where the view is
part of the living scheme, glass is the favored material for windbreaks. Transparent windscreens are
also popular for houses located on a windy hilltop
or the rim of an arroyo where updrafts swirl
through the outdoor living areas. A glass screen is
welcome alongside a swimming pool where it per-
mits the sun to dry the resting swimmers, but keeps
the wind from chilling them.

In small gardens, wherever summer heat is not a
problem, glass walls give wind protection without
loss of sunshine. And if privacy is needed, obscure
glass should be used.

PRO AND CON

Windscreens of glass are expensive and, in most
cases, no project for an amateur to undertake. As
everyone knows, glass is a fragile construction material. It will bend slightly under steady pressure,
but it is too rigid to withstand wrenching or jerking.
Consequently, a glass windscreen must be built
solidly to resist the buffeting of the wind or any
shifting of the soil. This requires careful and in-
formed designing—a professional's job—and stanch
construction.

Unlike most types of fences, a glass screen often
forces its prospective owner to study the habits of
his neighbors, cast a jaundiced eye upon the activities of their children—and his. A hard-driven baseball, an over-shot arrow, or a pellet from an air rifle
can make short work of a glass panel. A person
would think twice before erecting a windscreen next
to the fairway of a golf course.

CONSTRUCTION POINTERS

Methods of construction vary according to expected wind velocity and relative soil stability.

Ernest Braun, Photo

Preserving a lovely view and controlling the sea breeze are ends achieved by using a glass fence like the one above

John Robinson, Photo

The use of blue glass in combination with board reduces the glare of the sun in this shelter without cutting off view

All types of glass screens require substantial foundations and strong posts and frames. For this reason, many of them are built on top of low masonry walls or anchored to heavy concrete foundations. Simplest method is to design the screen as an extension of the house wall, using the house as one anchor point and deeply-embedded posts for the other.

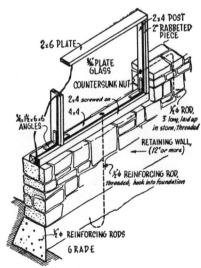

A glass screen can be damaged by warping of the posts and frames. This can usually be prevented by

using kiln-dried lumber and keeping it painted to protect it from the weather. Steel support posts and frames provide strong support, do not warp, and block off less scenery than heavy wooden framing.

It is advisable to use standard-sized glass panes. They are less expensive to buy and install than off-sizes, and they are more easily replaced when broken. In an emergency, the homeowner can replace them himself because they require no skilled cutting.

A screen built of a checkerboard of, say, 2-foot-square panes is often stronger than one made of large panels because of the large amount of framing, and if damaged, the injury is localized and less costly to repair. Whatever the size of the glass panes used, they should not be set into the fence so firmly that their replacement requires dismantling the structure. Usual practice is to attach them with rabbeted or square molding strips.

Weight of glass chosen should be heavy enough to take buffeting by the wind and survive an occasional collision by a low-flying bird. Double-weight window glass or ⅛-inch plate is adequate for installations with panes no larger than 24 x 36 inches. For larger panels, use ¼-inch plate, or, if clear vision is secondary, crystal glass. If glare is a prob-

Above left: A glass wall topped with a wind deflector faces ocean. The panels are 6 feet 6 inches, the deflector 1 foot

Above: Plate glass above fence admits sun, excludes wind. Solid fence in this limited space would have been too heavy

Center left: Patio is sheltered from the wind by a glass wall which mirrors plants in front of it, preserves view of hills

Below and left: Patio of this house faces ocean. Glass wind screen is bolted to flagstone wall with reinforcing rods, is high enough to stop ocean breezes without cutting off the view. In small gardens, wherever summer heat is not a problem, glass walls give wind protection without loss of sun

lem, it can be solved by using glare-reducing varieties of clear glass, such as blue glass; or if the view is expendable, obscure glasses, such as wire glass, pebble grain, louver grain, or the special heat-absorbing glass.

For a tough, boy-proof screen, you can consider the case-hardened glasses developed for solid glass doors and used for baseball backstops. It is obtainable in standard glass thicknesses, but it is quite expensive and must be ordered from the factory. If you can get it, small squares of automobile safety glass might merit consideration.

Lytton & Whitney, Design; Philip Fein, Photo

Center left: Molded glass panels have distinctive texture. Add interest here by their unusual staggered arrangement

Mason Weymouth, Photo

Center right: Original wall around this garden was increased by adding 30 inches of opaque skylight glass, bolted to wall

William Aplin, Photo

Lower left: Obscure glass added to shelter gives great privacy, still admits all the light necessary for the plants in flower bed

John Robinson, Photo

Lower right: Glass partition, used to separate garden sections, has a rough pebbled surface giving some privacy, ample light

Lawrence Halprin, Design; Childress-Halberstadt, Photo

Pampas grass is used with excellent effect against this fence of redwood posts with two- by four-inch caps, strung with wire

The light tracery of the wire carries out the delicate theme of the grass, while the dark wood makes an interesting silhouette

WIRE . . . highly practical and lasting

Many forms of wire fencing are more economical and longer-lived than wooden fencing. When security is the primary need, to confine pets or children and restrain intruders, wire is a superior material. With imaginative design, it can be used as a living fence, covered over with vines. It lends itself to quick and economical boundary fencing, where appearance is secondary. It is useful for intra-lot fencing, as around a vegetable plot, a kennel, the edge of a sundeck, or the rim of a swimming pool.

TYPES OF WIRE FENCES

The homeowner can choose between two general types of wire fence.

Wire and wood—Commonest type is the simple combination of wire mesh attached to wooden posts, such as the familiar line fence that you see rimming country fields and pastures. With rails added, it can be developed more interestingly: as shown in the drawing, strands of wire may be combined with a post-and-board type; or the framing may be designed to harmonize

Eckbo, Royston & Williams, Design; Childress-Halberstadt, Photo

This unusual screen is used primarily for decorative purposes and makes a semi-barrier between steps and sand pit

(62)

with the geometric pattern of the wire mesh. This variety often does double duty as a trellis for plantings.

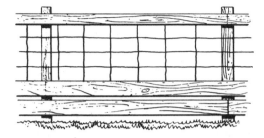

The pattern and weight of the wire you select depend upon the design and degree of security you need. Some of the available choices are shown on the next page.

Posts used with wood-and-mesh fences can either be squared lumber obtainable from the dealer, or round, peeled logs made from timber cut on the site. If squared posts are used, the choice of wood is the same as for any other type of fence, but if round posts are used, the selection is wide open. Many varieties of wood that never turn up in the lumber yard make excellent fence posts if they are properly treated with preservatives. Recommended woods are: redwood, cedar, cypress, oak, catalpas, madrone.

All-steel fences—All-steel fences are manufactured as complete units. The buyer is provided with posts, rails, mesh, gates, hinges, and other fittings.

All-steel fencing is ideal for keeping children and pets confined, for the patterns ordinarily used are hard

to climb. Aesthetically, it is not an appealing fence, and its graceful absorption into the garden plan presents a real challenge.

Mesh for this type of fence comes in two styles: the woven picket and the chain link. The former is less expensive and somewhat lighter than the latter. Both types come in rolls or cut strips 36, 42, and 48 inches in height. Chain link is also obtainable in larger sizes. Price of the mesh depends on the gauge of wire used. For chain link, 11-gauge is satisfactory for home use, but it is obtainable in 9- and 6-gauge for heavier duty. Both varieties are galvanized; one type of chain link is galvanized after the mesh has been woven, and is more rustproof than the variety that is dipped prior

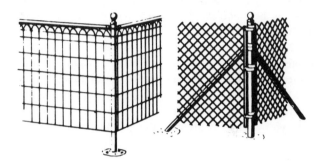

to weaving. Chain link is also manufactured from aluminum wire which does not rust. In some parts of the country you can get steel chain link fencing which

Eckbo, Royston & Williams, Design; M. Halberstadt, Photo

Open trellis serves as partial screen between entrance of this house and inner lawn area. Vines will cover eventually

Steel chain link fence interwoven with redwood pickets is more harmonious residential fence than plain link variety

is interwoven with redwood pickets. This design provides maximum security, yet is more acceptable in a back yard setting than the plain chain link, which tends to make your yard feel like a baseball grandstand behind home plate.

Posts are provided in two styles: round or channeled into **U** or **H**-shape cross section. The channeled posts are used only as line posts, the round ones as either corner or line posts. If a connecting rail is installed with the fence, round posts alone are used. Posts average 2 inches in diameter; connecting rails 1⅜ inches.

CONSTRUCTION POINTERS

Construction of a wire fence is within the capacity of a skilled handyman who can follow directions carefully, but it is a project that is best completed by two persons. As a rule, installation of a long stretch of chain-link fence is best entrusted to a contractor who specializes in their construction.

The main difficulty that will trouble the amateur is stretching the fence wire taut. This requires special devices and presents some hazard to an inexperienced builder. A long length of fencing may require a pull of several hundred pounds to get it to proper tension.

If you decide to attempt the job yourself, send for the U. S. Department of Agriculture Farmer's Bulletin, 1832, "Farm Fences" for instructions.

Here are the principal steps in building wire fences.

Setting posts—Posts are ordinarily spaced 10 feet apart. If wooden posts are used, set them in place as if for a wooden fence, as outlined elsewhere in this book.

Steel post installation depends on whether the post is round or channeled. The tubular posts should always be set in concrete. Bore an 8-inch hole 2 feet deep, set post in it, and fill in with the concrete; or, fill the hole with concrete and shove the post down into it. True the post with a level.

Channeled posts are usually driven into soil. Use special sleeve-type driver made for this purpose, or pound them down with a sledge, taking care to protect the top of the post with a block of wood. If a driven post strikes rock, withdraw the post so it won't become bent. Remove the stone or shift the post.

Corner posts are braced to withstand the pull of the wire. Dig a vertical hole for the end of the brace that enters the ground, fill it with concrete, shove one end of the brace into it, and attach the other to the post with the special clamps provided.

STRETCHING WIRE FENCE

All wire fencing should be stretched before it is permanently fastened to the posts. This is the tricky part of the job. For a short fence, brute strength may suffice, but for longer fences, use a block and tackle, a manufactured fence stretcher, or a borrowed truck or jeep.

Paul Lazlo, Design; Julius Shulman, Photo

Above: A fence for keeping children confined, chain mesh is successfully absorbed into garden plan by use of plantings

Left: In the panel are shown nine of the more common types of wire, mesh, and screen available for use in open fencing

Unroll about 25 feet of wire along the ground, with one end next to a corner post. Stand it up and fasten it securely to the post. Continue unrolling

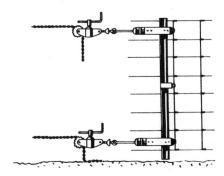

until the end of the roll is reached or a point where the mesh is to be cut, as at a corner post. Fasten a heavy pipe, bar, or strong piece of wood to the free end of the wire, and attach the pulling device to it. If you use a block and tackle, anchor it to a tree or an automobile, but not to a fence post.

If you attach the pulling rope to a truck, apply tension slowly, and when wire is taut, set the brakes. When the slack is all pulled out of the wire, attach the mesh to the posts before releasing the pull. Amateurs usually stretch wire too loosely, but it should not be pulled so tight that it will not be able to contract in cold weather.

On long fences, two rolls can be stretched at the same time by attaching them to posts at the opposite ends of the line. Usually, wire mesh should be cut so the end just overlaps a post, but if it is necessary to end a stretch between posts, it can be spliced to the next roll (a job requiring skill). Wire should not be pulled around a corner. On curved fences, it must be brought around in a series of short, straight lengths. (For information about bringing wire under tension around a curve, write to Ohio Agricultural Experiment Station, Wooster, Ohio, for Research Circular 5, *Contour Fencing*.) If the fence runs up and down dale, stretch it from the points where it changes grade.

UTILITY FENCING

If you need an economical or temporary fence, you may want to use the so-called "utility fence," a variety of picket fence that is manufactured in roll form.

Utility fencing consists of dressed and painted pickets that are held in alignment by strands of galvanized wire, twisted between each picket. They are obtainable in natural finish, or in white, green, or red, with squared or pointed tops. They are sold in 2-, 3-, and 4-foot heights, in 50- and 100-foot rolls.

To install utility fencing:

1. Set posts and top and bottom rails, as outlined in the construction chapter. The lower rail is often omitted.
2. Unroll the fence on the ground alongside the posts.
3. Stand the fence against the posts and staple one end against the first post with a gun stapler.
4. Stretch the fence taut and staple it to the next post, using a board as a lever to tighten it. Insert the board through the fence next to the post, and, using the post as a fulcrum, pull the fence tight and straight.
5. When the fence has been attached to the last post, staple the top wire to the top rail.

Most utility fencing is not made of decay-resistant wood and should therefore be kept from touching the ground. A baseboard will strengthen the fence and keep the pickets free of the ground.

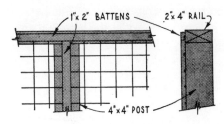

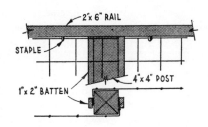

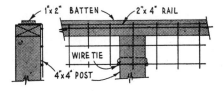

Battens, staples, or strands of wire are mainstays for attaching wire mesh to fence frames. Illustrations shown demonstrate five different fastenings fence builders use to solve this problem

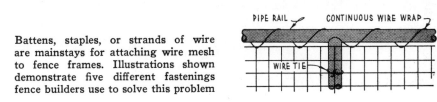

Mimi Bell, Photo

The familiar, sometimes meandering country fence is boundary line marker, and keeps livestock under control. This model is woven wire with two barbed strands above it

COUNTRY FENCES ... by the acre

Out in the country—even on a one or two-acre place —a fence still has the significance it had in our grandfathers' day: it excludes unwanted livestock and other creatures, it holds in your own animals, and it preserves local harmony. The city dweller's considerations of privacy, space division, and outdoor living don't mean much in the rural setting where you have a half-mile between you and your neighbor, and are fencing acres instead of feet.

Economic factors alone dictate that country fencing is more open and less decorative than what you'd find in a subdivision. Barbed wire and woven wire are the standard, multipurpose materials in rural areas. There are also situations that call for specialized materials— chain link for maximum security, electric fences for pasturing livestock, post-and-rail for looks (see chapter on rail fences), and board fences for corrals.

BARBED WIRE

Barbed wire is the most economical of the multi-purpose fences. Like all country fencing it's sold by the rod, which is 16½ feet. If an acre is square it measures 12½ rods on each side. Price for barbed wire depends on the gauge of wire, the number of barbs (two or four points), and barb spacing, usually four or five inches apart. Inexpensive, light-weight wire is 14-gauge; the more costly, heavy-duty type is 12½ gauge. Both types are heavily galvanized.

Barbed wire can injure children and tear clothing, so it isn't satisfactory near the house. It's best used to hold livestock in large, open-country fields.

WOVEN WIRE

This type of fencing, also called field fence and stock fence, comes in 10 and 20-rod rolls or bales. The horizontal line wires are spaced narrower at the bottom than at the top to keep out small animals. Vertical stay wires are spaced 6 or 12 inches apart. Woven wire is standardized within five sizes: You can get 7, 8, 9, 10, or 11 line wires in heights of 26, 32, 39, 47, and 55 inches. The 47-inch size with 10 line wires is probably the best choice for fencing several acres. It is high and strong enough to stop all domestic animals. Some poultry fences are made in the same pattern, but generally of lighter wire (11 to 15½ gauge), higher (36 to 72 inches), and with more line wires (19, 20, 21, and 23). It's made for poultry but will resist livestock in temporary fencing situations.

Good grades of woven wire have tension curves or crimps in the line wires between each stay. These

Actual size gauge measures of the wires used in fencing. Usual range: 11–14½

crimps allow for contraction and expansion when the temperature changes. One type of woven wire has squares of the same size all the way down. It comes in both 6-foot and 3-foot heights.

POULTRY NETTING

This is lightweight (20 gauge) wire formed into square or hexagonal mesh. Even under ideal support and tension, it's only strong enough to pen up poultry, though it discourages small animals from entering the hen yard. The material serves well for a short time around small yards, but for better service get woven wire poultry fencing.

You can buy hexagonal poultry netting in one-inch and two-inch mesh. The smaller type is recommended for chicks, comes in heights between 18 and 72 inches. Two-inch mesh starts at 36 inches high, goes up to 72 inches. It's available either galvanized before or after weaving. The latter, more rustproof, costs about one and a half times as much as the type that is galvanized before weaving.

STEEL CHAIN LINK

For a strong practically indestructible fence that requires little upkeep and cannot be climbed, nothing beats a steel chain link fence. Compared with other fencing, however, it's expensive—enclosing an acre would cost from $200 up. The high initial cost is balanced by the long life of the fence. It should last a lifetime, while other types take replacement about every 20 years. Steel or aluminum chain link fences are particularly good for enclosing house yards, play areas, pump houses, and water supplies.

ELECTRIC

The value of an electric fence is a matter of controversy. In its favor: it requires only one strand of wire and can be shifted easily or installed temporarily to protect crops from stock, or to control grazing. In its disfavor: under some circumstances, it presents a serious shock hazard, particularly to children; it requires constant maintenance—weeds ground it, must be cut back constantly; loose connections develop that reduce its efficiency, cause radio interference; stock must be educated to respect it, otherwise they will saunter right through it; and if current fails, part or all of an entire

fence loses its value. However, there are thousands of satisfied owners. Most states have laws governing these fences. Before you install one, talk to manufacturers, your county agent, and the local power or public utilities representative.

THE "ALL-PURPOSE" FENCE

No one type of fencing can be classed as *the* all-purpose fence. The best fence, of course, is the one that works in terms of your specific problem. For instance, a sheep raiser troubled with dogs might resort to the fence shown below. The rodent proof fence on this page is nothing like the deer stoppers illustrated at the end of the chapter.

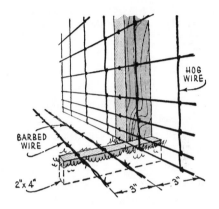

However, there are practical minimums in fencing, and some agreement on the types that hold the greatest variety of animals. In the agricultural statutes of one Western state, the bare minimum fence is described like this: "No wire fence is a good substantial fence unless it has three tightly stretched barbed wires securely fastened to posts of reasonable strength, firmly

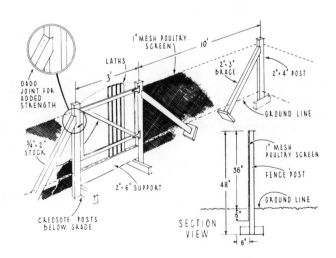

Rodent-resistant fence is galvanized mesh, 3 feet high; extends into soil 6 inches. Underground shelf adds 6 inches

planted in the ground no more than one rod apart. One of the wires shall be at least four feet above the surface of the ground. Any kind of wire or other fence equal to or greater in height, strength, or capacity than the wire fence described is a good and substantial fence."

Woven wire stock and field fence—the type that is 47 inches high with 10 strands—by itself, or topped with a strand of barbed wire, will hold the greatest variety of animals. Such a fence must be made taut, or livestock will ride it with their necks, making it sag and perhaps fall down.

If your fence is to hold only sheep and other small animals, you can cut costs by erecting a smaller size woven wire fence—for instance the 26-inch size—with three barbed wires above, or a 32-inch fence with two strands of barbed wire above it.

FENCE POSTS

For stringing any of these fences you have a choice of steel, wood, or concrete posts. Except for the fact that rural fencing is usually on a larger scale than city fencing, the problems of setting posts in the ground are the same. Fences will rot, blow down, and burn in either environment. Briefly, here are some points to consider:

Steel posts drive easily, particularly in rocky soils where digging post holes would be difficult. Steel is fireproof and can be moved more easily than other posts. At the same time, steel posts cost more than wood posts of the same height, and the metal will bend under high winds. Lifetime is about the same as wood that has been treated—figure on 20 years.

Wood posts are a natural choice if you have a timber source on your property. They are more compatible with the rural scene and comparatively inexpensive. Nevertheless, you'll have to treat most wood with preservative to prevent rot, and the cost gets higher as you get away from the lumber country.

Concrete posts have a great advantage over both steel and wood in longevity. Make your forms and pour your posts yourself. Use them at corners and for bracing a line of metal or wood posts. Set galvanized nails in the posts before they harden, points out, for fastening the fence. There's no moving the posts, once they're in. For more information on setting and preserving fence posts, see the technical chapters at the back of the book.

DEER FENCING

Keeping deer out of an orchard or garden calls for some special fencing measures. Regular stock fences of barbed wire do not exclude deer because they crawl between the strands.

A high fence is the most effective way to keep them out, usually you go to 8 feet using two 4-foot strips of 14-gauge woven wire poultry fence. Fences should be higher in regions where snow piles up during winter months. If deer come over low fences in just certain spots, you might try installing 8-foot outriggers in these positions, because deer are poor broad jumpers. In real problem cases, put a wire overhang on top of an 8-foot fence facing outward at a 45-degree angle.

If you are considering a deer fence, check with your state Game Commission. Some states will finance a part or all of the cost of deer fencing for landowners suffering deer damage, provided the fence is built to state specifications.

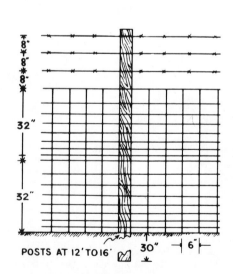

Economical deer fence 7½ feet high, made of two 32-inch rolls of poultry fencing, topped with 3 barbed strands

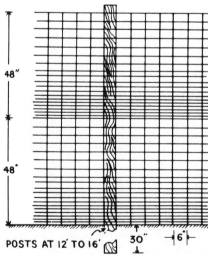

Two 4-foot strips of 14 gauge poultry fencing more secure against deer who often get through barbed wire fences

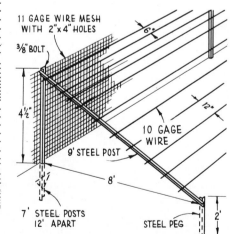

Use outriggers to foil the deer where you want to keep your fence low for a view. The outriggers are steel posts

CORRALS... horses' well being comes first

The good horseman considers the well being of his horses *first* in building a fence. He avoids barbed wire for obvious reasons. Smooth wire also has its dangers, particularly when the horse is shod; he may catch the wire between shoe and hoof, and, in jerking back, which he instinctively does, he will tighten the wire's grip, ending up with a badly wrenched leg or shoulder.

Wood gives the best over-all results, with rails or boards parallel to the ground and nailed to the inside of the posts to remove the danger of a horse hitting his shoulder on a post as he gallops by. A flat board top from post to post will prolong the life of the fence by keeping off the sun and rain,

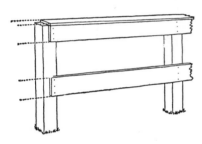

besides acting as a brace. Slanted boards will shed the rain better, but many horse owners will settle for a flat top on which they can perch to watch the horses.

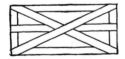

Using **X**-braces on gates for horses, as shown above, should be avoided. A pawing horse can get his hoof caught in the intersection. If he pulls the

wrong way, which he usually does, he will tighten up on the trapped hoof with the possible result of another lame horse.

Means should be taken to block off, or round, the fence corners, particularly if there is to be more than one horse in the pasture. Loose horses usually

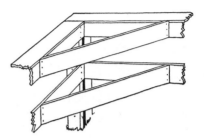

are kicked when they have been chased and cornered by the bully in the group.

Pasture gates, large enough to admit a truck, should be placed for the most convenience so that they swing in or out. Some prefer the out-swinging type, like a stall door. With a gate that opens into the pasture, a horse is likely to hit a hip on the free end if he succeeds in starting through as you close it. This is a particular hazard with more than one horse in the pasture: trying to shut a gate by pulling it toward you when the horse you don't want is half-way through, and the horse you do want is fouling the lead rope trying to get back in, may mean injury to a horse, and, certainly, to your aplomb.

Hip injuries to horses may be further avoided by placing the gate at a corner of the pasture so that it closes directly against the sideboards and so that there is no projection against which a crowded horse might lurch.

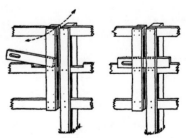

Above is an effective gate latch which can be made by nailing a board with cleats on its post-side to the inside of the gate post and slipping a slat, or even a stout stick, through the cleats and between the gate uprights.

Gates may be fitted with a horseman's latch, one that can be tripped by a mounted rider, who lifts the latch with his foot or works an extension handle.

A steel rod, with a turnbuckle in the middle to permit adjustments, as shown above, will help to keep a gate from sagging.

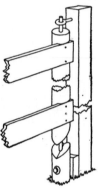

Self-closing gate hinges are a convenience, but you must provide some means to hook the gate back when you want it to stand open.

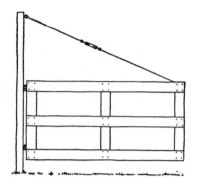

EMERGENCY GATE

There are more ways of getting through a fence than by swinging open a hinged gate. Where en-trance is only occasional, a gate can be built to slide out of the way, a stretch of barbed wire can be un-hooked, or a stile can be built to let a person climb

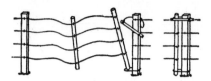

over the fence. A baffle pass-through can be fitted into it, large enough to pass people and dogs but too small for horses or cattle. A turnstile is also effective, but should not be used in a stock fence because it will injure horses or cattle.

A MOVABLE PASTURE FENCE

A type of fence you may find handy with horses, or for a variety of purposes, is the movable pasture fence. A single section, such as the one illustrated, would be approximately 16 feet long and 4 feet high. A number of these can be used in combination to form riding rings, temporary corrals and pas-tures, and as chutes to load horses on trucks. They

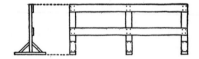

are handy when both time and help are short. Fas-ten the sections together with hay wire at top, cen-ter and bottom of the end uprights. This type of fence naturally is not as strong as a permanent one with posts embedded in the ground, but it is sur-prisingly practical.

Eckbo, Royston & Williams, Design; Morley Baer, Photo

Five-foot high fence of 2 by 4's with welded wire between uprights makes handsome barrier. Mesh has 1 by 2 vertical pattern which is hard to climb. Access to pool is through large gates at either end of the pool, which can be locked

POOL ENCLOSURES...where security matters

Owning an open swimming pool can be compared with keeping a pet tiger—it's a lot of fun, but once in a while it does away with one of the neighborhood children. The problem of keeping small children away from unguarded private pools has reached the point where some cities have ordinances prohibiting unprotected pools.

Legal considerations aside, most pool owners want pool protection just for their own peace of mind when they are away from home. There are three ways to safeguard your pool—a permanent lifeguard, a pool cover, or a fence. Most pool owners choose fencing. A lifeguard is impractical except for supervised swimming. Chances are he won't be on duty at night which leaves the pool unguarded. Though many cities regard a pool cover equal to a fence security wise, most people feel it's too much trouble to uncover the pool every time they want a swim.

What are the considerations in fencing a swimming pool? Security is the most important factor; here are some points to consider:

Decide what age group you want to keep out. Tod-

Ernest Wertheim, Design; Mason Weymouth, Photo

Vertical board fence topped with plastic screen panels provides privacy, wind control, keeps pool area light, cheerful

W. Bennett Covert, Design

When pool is unsupervised, three 8-foot gate sections of steel chain link fence close off swimming area completely

When pool is in use, the gates swing back to create a full 24-foot opening, so that pool appears to be totally unfenced

Ernest Braun, Photo

A rustic 6-foot grapestake fence is just right backdrop for irregularly-shaped pool that is surrounded by flagstone deck

dlers and small children are usually safe behind a 4½-foot fence as long as the gate latch is out of reach.

Sometimes even a 6-foot fence won't keep out older children who are determined to get in, but the higher fence with a locking latch presents a visual barrier that discourages all but the most athletic trespassers.

Any pool security fence should be made without horizontal toe-holds. A 4-inch mesh, for instance, provides just about the right toe space for junior brogans. Metal mesh should not be over 2 inches wide horizontally, and there should be no horizontal fence stringers or supports that could be climbed like a ladder. Louver and basket weave fences should be avoided. You should also be able to see through the pool fence from the house and patio. When you hear a splash, you want to see what made it.

DESIGN

Though security is the primary objective of pool fencing, don't overlook the design elements. There's no need to turn your pool area into a prison compound. Use plantings and decorative effects to help the fence blend into the landscape. Chain link fences, for example, which provide maximum security, are easy to mask with vines.

Morley Baer, Photo

The back of this lath overhead is a 6-foot grapestake fence. Vines growing on fence have reached the overhead structure.

Combination creates a warm sheltered pocket that is out of wind and protected from slanting rays of the afternoon sun

If your yard is completely enclosed by a boundary fence, you may decide you have adequate pool protection. However, there are some powerful arguments for fencing the immediate pool area:

A boundary fence will screen out the neighborhood children, but it won't protect the toddlers in your own family. When you fence near the pool you keep most of the leaves and dirt from blowing into the water, thus reducing pool maintenance. A poolside fence provides more specific climate control since you can orient the panels to block out chilling winds and create sun pockets that make swimming more enjoyable. This is especially important when you're sitting around in a wet swimsuit. It's probably best to arrange your fence to admit the afternoon sun, because you do more swimming at that time of day.

Finally, by fencing the pool you separate and define the area devoted to swimmers. It's often possible to control the dressing room and lavatory traffic with fence panels, screening it away from the living room. A solid fence can provide the back wall for a dressing room or a pool cabana. Don't overlook the possibility of using a single panel or a short free-standing fence to hide unsightly filtration and heating equipment.

Ruth Patricia Shellhorn, Design; William Aplin, Photo

A glass windscreen shelters swimmers and preserves view of distant hills. Security fence is located on lower ground

Margaret Sullivan, Design; William Aplin, Photo

Above left: Free-standing woven picket fence is used to hide filtration equipment, create a sun pocket, and display plants

Eckbo, Royston & Williams, Design

Above: A light post-and-rail fence borders deck overhanging pool. For more security you can install mesh between rails

Julius Shulman, Photo

Center: A steel chain link gate on rollers closes off this pool. It can be rolled back to leave one end of the pool wide open

Henry Hill, Design; Morley Baer, Photo

Below left: This pool demonstrates ultimate in security. A heavy wood frame and welded mesh completely enclose pool

MacBird and Associates, Design; George de Gennaro, Photo

Below: Property line slat fence forms the back of this pool shelter and dressing room. Note repetition of slat pattern

Robert Cornwall, Design; Phil Palmer, Photo

Vines on this horizontal fence extend level of the lawn, and screen out near views of road and neighbors below. Wires strung between frame support plantings

HORIZONTAL FENCING . . . for hillside privacy

To make the horizontal fence above look more like a conventional fence, you may have to turn the book a quarter turn counter-clockwise. However, in function, if not in appearance, this type of fencing is very similar to its vertical brothers.

The only place a horizontal fence will work is on a hillside lot, where it solves some special problems. Most people buying hillside lots are interested in the scenic views such property affords. But after they move in, they discover that along with the far vistas they have a disconcerting shorter view into the yards or living rooms of their neighbors below. Furthermore, living on a hill is something like living on a stage. When the incline is gradual, your neighbors and the passing traffic below have a front row seat at all your front yard activities.

In this situation, a conventional fence would provide privacy, but blot out the scenic distant views. A horizontal fence shuts out the objectionable part of the near landscape and preserves your scenery. To be a true horizontal fence, it should be open—just a framework to support shrubs and vines. If you use solid materials, your fence is then called a deck.

William Aplin, Photo

Topside view shows function of horizontal fence. Without it, hilltop patio would have direct view into neighbor's yard

(75)

A combination of lattice and plain board gives a solid but friendly look to this entrance way. Lightness of wood emphasized by bricks

GATES . . . build for wear and abuse

A gate is more than a square of wood attached to a fence by a pair of hinges. Often it tells something about the people who live in the house beyond it. A front gate, for instance, is the first thing your visitors encounter. Before they even touch the latch the gate makes a visual impression—either inviting or forbidding, formal or informal, romantic or functional.

And everyone who uses your gates, both guests and delivery men, will notice little details in construction that tell them something about you. Does the gate seem solid? Does it swing freely or agonizingly? Does the latch work smoothly and effectively? Is the gate simple, straightforward, and in keeping with the house and garden, or does it seem to be out of character?

DESIGN

Generally speaking, you put in a gate because you have to get through a fenced area, so its design dictates to some extent the design of the gate. By using the same materials, you can make the gate blend right into the fence. Side yard gates are usually of this type because most home owners don't want anything more elaborate in this location.

By altering the design slightly—changing the spacing of the siding used on the gate, for example—you can make the gate stand out without creating a sharp contrast with the fence. When you use completely different materials on the gate, it becomes a focal point, and relegates the fence to second place.

Gates should harmonize with the architectural tone of your house, inside and out. The visitor passing through a formal, Williamsburg picket gate would be unprepared for a severe, modern living room; so would a person opening a grapestake gate be unprepared for a Victorian living room.

The size of the gate is determined by the height of

the fence it serves, and according to the degree of security you want. It should be in scale with its surroundings. A low, inadequate front gate is an annoyance, and a challenge to budding young hurdlers. Oversize gates, on the other hand, may seem ostentatious or institutional in character.

Some gates, of course, defy or don't leave you much originality in design. The ones that come to you complete from the factory are only as adaptable as the range of plans in the catalog. Gates that serve strictly utilitarian purposes, such as those that close the pasture, orchard, or barnyard, look their best in honest workaday situations.

But, ornate or simple, high or low, owner-built or prefabricated, all gates must meet one common requirement—they have to work.

PLANNING

Gates take a beating. They get more wear and abuse than any other part of the fence, and if they are expected to last, they must be built solidly and attached with top quality, heavy-duty hardware. When you put in a header board along a path, or nail lath on a trellis, you can make a small error here and there, and no one will know the difference. But a few miscalculations or a little bad workmanship on a gate, and you end up with one

that doesn't close; or worse, one that won't open in wet weather.

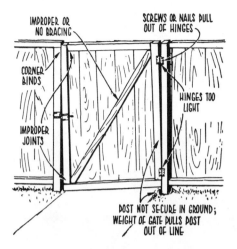

To avoid these pitfalls, plan your gate carefully. A good first step, particularly if the project is complex, is to make a sketch of your proposed gate and show it to your lumber dealer. He can usually tell you whether your plan is feasible, how much it will cost, and whether there's some way to make the job easier by modifying the design slightly. Before you make a sketch, however, you'll have to know something about gate construction.

This solid, wooden gate with iron fixtures is carved with intricate floral pattern on left; also, carving on crossbar

A light lattice gate breaks up solid lines of the board fence, and seems to be more inviting than a heavy, ornate gate

Sliding wooden bolt works well on gate made of split bamboo. Conventional latch would be hard to mount on poles

There are three considerations: the latch, the hinges, and the gate itself.

LATCHES

Although it may seem like putting the cart before the horse, the first thing to consider is the latch. In many cases you have to build the gate around the latch, unless it's a simple hasp or hook. For example, a sliding bolt action latch may be too difficult to install on a gate with grapestake siding. Check hardware and lumber supply stores for latch ideas. Some of the common designs are shown on this page, or you can have more ornate latches made to order. Wooden latches, designed as part of the gate, are fun to devise, do not rust, and are easily replaced if they wear out or break.

Remember that the latch must take rough treatment. A flimsy one, put on with small nails or screws, won't last long. If you want to keep the small fry from opening the gate, get a latch that you can set up high or on top of the fence.

HINGES

The principal cause of gate failure is inadequate hinges. Err on the side of ruggedness to take care of eventualities such as garden gate swingers.

Hinges, like latches, have to be considered in terms of the gate siding. It would be impossible, for example, to mount heavy strap hinges on a gate paneled in translucent plastic. Sometimes you'll want to buy hinges that

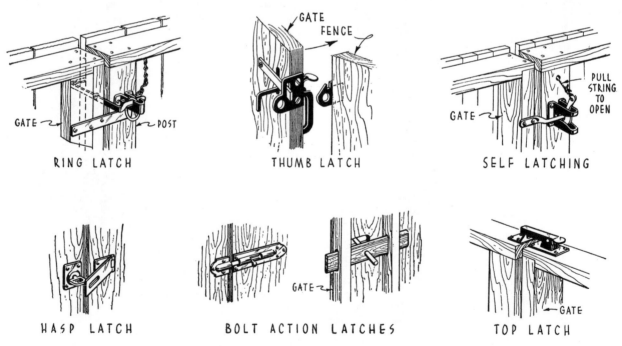

These are the latches most hardware stores carry as regular stock. Use hasp latch for maximum security, variety of the thumb latch in cases where appearance is important. Ring and self-latching models catch even when gate is slammed

match your latch, which may call for a revision in your gate design. When your fence is used to confine small children, self-closing hinges are a worthwhile investment. Springs in the hinge mechanism automatically close one gate, which otherwise might be left ajar by visitors or deliverymen.

Some of the more familiar hinges are illustrated below. All of them do a good job, providing they are sized for the weight of the gate, and if you use screws that are long enough. Many of the packaged hinges include screws that are too short for a heavy gate. Use screws that go as far into the wood as possible, without coming out the other side. Always use three hinges on gates that are over 5 feet tall. Buy only hinges with a weather-resistant coating—cadmium, zinc, or galvanized—unless you plan on painting them; otherwise they'll rust and streak your gate.

MATERIALS

In selecting the material for your gate, you have the same choices as in fence siding. Most gates have 2 by 4-inch frames, covered with facing material. You can use lighter frames if the siding is exterior plywood or some other light material. These won't sag, but they usually need support on the flat sides to keep them from bowing, and to give you a place to fasten hinges and latches. Don't buy warped lumber. It doesn't take much of a curve to throw the whole gate out of line. Sometimes you may have to go through half a dozen pieces before

A. L. Francis, Photo

Above: Hospitable white gate uses wide boards on sides, narrow board in center. Distinctive metal trim and gate handle

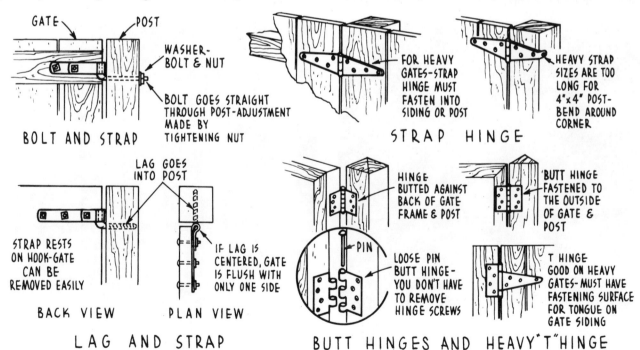

The familiar hinges shown are offered in wide range of sizes. Most gates need heavy-duty models. Bolt and lag hinges let gate swing either way, require strong latch. Use butt hinges when gate facing will not accommodate hinge straps

1. Gate builder had to fit gate into an existing opening. It's easier to set the hinge post, then build gate and set latch post after gate is hung on hinge post

2. The ground slopes so measurements are taken on level board between posts. Top of the gate is level with fence; bottom line follows the sloping walk

3. Build frame on level ground, check fit in opening; make adjustments before installing the brace. All frame members are 2 by 4's; joints mortised

you get a straight one. If you have to buy green lumber, let it dry out for at least a week before you use it. Lay the boards on blocks to let the air circulate around the wood.

BUILDING THE GATE

Usually you build a gate to fit a predetermined hole in the fence. Make sure the passage is wide enough to handle the traffic of garden carts and such—three feet is a minimum opening. There's nothing more irritating than a skimpy gate opening that means skinned knuckles every time you push a wheelbarrow through it. Gates that border a sidewalk or highway should open inward.

Your fence posts should be firmly imbedded, as discussed elsewhere in this book, to withstand the pull of the gate. When possible attach the hinge post to the house wall for added support. To measure the opening, take your measurements at top and bottom. If there's a considerable difference you'll have to make your posts plumb before you can hang a gate between them.

The normal construction sequence is to build your frame, install the bracing, add siding, hang the gate,

A see-through gate is an open invitation into garden beyond. Scroll-sawn design complements brick wall on either side

When this gate is closed, it blends right in with remainder of fence. The panels are 1 by 12's; the battens are 2 by 2's

4. Set wood brace from top of latch post to bottom of hinge post. Work will be more accurate if gate is built flat on ground, not upright as shown

5. A turnbuckle and a wire which run from top of hinge post to the foot of latch post is alternate brace. Metal straps or screw eyes hold wire in place

6. Siding can go on frame before you hang the gate or afterward. This gate has rough 1 by 2 siding and top latch. The posts are 4 by 4's set in concrete

and put on the latch. You can hang the gate before the siding goes on if the complete gate is too heavy to be manageable.

Assuming you are using the standard 2 by 4 frame and 4 by 4-inch posts, first measure the distance between the posts. Leave at least ½ to ¾ inch between the latch post and the gate frame, so your gate can swing without binding. If you're not handy at keeping track of fractions and other measurements, use a straight 1 by 1-inch garden stake as a guide. Holding it level between the gate posts, mark off the latch post, swing space, gate

frame member, hinge space, and the hinge post. You can build the gate frame using this as your only guide.

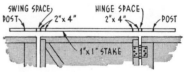

Make sure you cut square corners on all frame members. Check the ends you don't cut as they're not always sawn square at the mill. Cut lap joints for all corners for strength. Redrill your nail and screw holes with a

Wide boards in gates carry out fence pattern. Double width is for cars, while the single gate at left is for foot traffic

Trellis gate for the traditional picket fence may be covered by vines. But they will have to be removed for repainting

There is little chance that this gate will ever sag. Note the three heavy strap hinges and sturdy diagonal support brace

Associated Photos

A low gate of wide, well-spaced boards inside the garden can effectively keep children corralled away from the adults

bit that's slightly smaller in diameter than the fasteners. Use galvanized or other treated hardware that won't corrode and discolor the face of your gate.

To prevent sagging, you should brace your gate

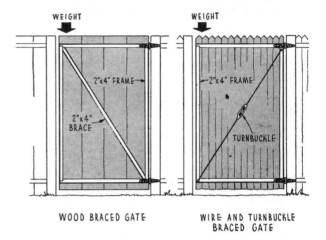

WOOD BRACED GATE   WIRE AND TURNBUCKLE BRACED GATE

frame. The most common brace is a 2 by 4 set diagonally from the bottom corner of the frame on the hinge post side to the top corner of the latch side. This actually pushes up the frame from the bottom of the hinge post; you can't do this by running a wood brace the opposite way and expect the gate not to sag. The amateur gate builder has a hard time getting this brace in place. Hold the 2 by 4 in place and mark the angle with a pencil. Be careful; if you're off 1/8 of an inch, you won't get a tight fit. After you cut the brace, if it doesn't fit snugly, tighten it up with a wedge.

Another good way to brace a gate is with a wire and turnbuckle, or a metal rod, diagonally in the opposite direction; that is, it goes from the top of the frame on the hinge side to the bottom on the latch side. This brace pulls up the frame to the top of the hinge post. You can buy sets containing wire, a turnbuckle, and two metal angle plates that fit over the edges of the gate frame. Or attach the wire to screw eyes set in the frame. A metal shop will make up rod and turnbuckle rigs to your specifications.

Wire or rod bracing has three advantages: It is easier and faster to install; it is easier to adjust if the gate sags; and it is not as bulky or heavy as a wood brace.

GATE REPAIR

What do you do when a new gate sags, binds, or won't latch? First, check the hinge post to see if it is still solid and plumb. If not, you will have to shore it up. Sometimes a wire from the hinge post to a more solid post down the line will correct the tilt. If the gate still binds, check hinges to see if they've pulled out

Alfred Preis, Design; W. M. Pitchford, Photo

Attractive entrance gate is faced with a light hardboard. The see-through mesh panels provide both design and ventilation

Jerry Anson, Photo

Set in solid frame of 2- by 8-inch lumber, the slender ribs of saguaro cactus make an effective fence top, an interesting gate

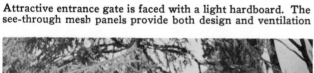

Angus McSweeney, Design; Mason Weymouth, Photo

Gate posts set in masonry wall above are fastened to wall by bolts which are sunk in mortar joints between the bricks

Howard B. Hoffman, Photo

Here is the versatile grapestake used in a gate. The vertical pickets are braced on back by a diagonal. Note uneven top

Thomas Church, Design; John Robinson, Photo

Above left: The wire gate and fence are physical rather than visual barriers. Diagonal brace marks the location of gate

Above: Chances are this gate will last indefinitely. The steel frame is bolted to concrete posts which are tied to the house

Center: The narrow pickets in gate harmonize with wider boards in fence, but subtly break up the march of pickets

Below left: Solid gate has top of boards cut jaggedly to make uneven line. This breaks up line of the wall, gives variety

a little. When posts and hinges are in good order, try tightening the turnbuckle, or wedging up the wood brace.

Often a sagging gate will not latch properly. Sometimes the whole gate post sinks slightly, causing the latch bar to miss the catch. Then you'll have to reset either the hinges or latch. If screws and nails pull out of the wood, remove the gate and hinges, fill the holes with a strong glue and reset the hinge when the glue is perfectly dry. Or change the location of the hinges using longer screws. Sometimes delivery men develop the habit of going through the gate without bothering to work the latch. If this happens they will probably tear the latch plate out unless screws go as far into the post as possible.

A gate may bind in wet weather and work like a charm when it's dry. In this case, plane off a little of the latch post or gate frame. You can frequently restore an old gate by simply replacing a wooden brace with a wire and turnbuckle brace.

Above: A traditional wrought iron gate matches lines of the fence. This fencing is quite expensive, hazardous to children

Burton Schutt, Design; George Szanik, Photo

Right: Chinese moon gate covered with bronze grill. The design is inviting, and is often used to frame a garden view

Morley Baer, Photo

The trim louvered gates match the clean, functional lines of wall, yet take away the unfriendly appearance of masonry

Note attention-getting arrangement of narrow redwood pieces in this oriental-type gate and fence. Eye is drawn to center

Figs espaliered on this fence have lush foliage in summer, reveal branch patterns against boards in winter. Heaviness of solid panels of 1 by 12-inch boards is lightened by alternate groups of spaced 1 by 4's which let the air circulate

FENCES and PLANTS...mutual admiration society

Even though you may have planned your fence to fit into your garden, it may occur to you when it is finished that you have a pretty long and monotonous expanse of lumber surrounding you. To break up this stark appearance, you will probably want to use some kind of vine or plants along the fence.

Plants and fences have a wonderful reciprocal relationship to one another. Plants help fences to become more a part of the landscape by softening the stern lines of the structure. You add new patterns, textures, and color accents to your existing fence according to the way it's planted. A planted fence is cooler, both in appearance and function, than one of bare boards. In extreme cases plantings can hide an unattractive fence completely.

A fence, in turn, focuses attention on the plants in front of it. It provides firm support that eliminates the need for staking plantings. It acts as a windbreak, creating a haven of quiet air on the lee side. A fence stores or reflects heat on its sunny side—even an open rail fence deflects the flow of freezing air that causes plant

In a year these newly planted evergreen elms will form a billowy green wave of foliage that will blot out line of fence

damage. On the north or east side of the house, shade-loving plants flourish behind the shelter of a fence.

Because of their mutual dependence, you have to consider fences and plants together in any planting scheme. It is impossible in a limited space to give a list of plants that would fit every climate and landscape, but here are some general points to guide you:

For light foliage effects against delicately constructed fences of wire mesh, plastic screen, thin lath, or bamboo stakes, use vines and shrubs that create a graceful pattern and are not too thick or heavy looking. If your fence has a distinctive pattern or finish, a heavy mass of green leaves and flowers will blot it out. Bear in mind that some plants are very sturdy, and the more pugna-

cious varieties can wrench apart a lightly constructed fence.

Against solid panels, board, and rough grapestakes use vines and shrubs that have large thick leaves or bushy masses of finer foliage. Dark, solid fences that seem too massive can be helped with low to medium plants in

the foreground using light, gray foliaged shrubs. A single solid panel makes a good backdrop for displaying

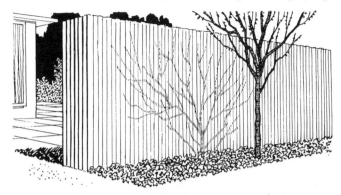

plants, particularly those that you want to highlight, or that might get lost if planted among other foliage. Even though you prefer evergreen plants, don't overlook the design value of bare winter branches followed by the refreshing effect of spring foliage.

In narrow planting spaces along a fence, espaliered shrubs are the logical choice. Fruit trees are especially popular in this situation—they are easy to control and you can grow them to yield a few special prizes. When your fence is exposed to the full rays of the sun, leave space between the fence and plants or they may burn in the reflected heat. In marginal citrus areas, fruit trees flourish in the shelter of some fences—glass and plastic hold heat particularly well.

Gravity works against you when you grow a plant

Wooden grid of 2 by 4's planted with grapevines that provide effective screen between outdoor living area and street

Espaliered variegated ivy twines on wires along board fence. The vine is about 10 years old, and requires monthly pruning

against a fence. You'll have to devise ways to help the plant stand up. Use soft, non-cutting materials to tie them—raffia, cloth, rubber strips, or coated wire are good. Supporting wires can be bare, but this wire may heat and burn tender shoots. Insulated wire or plastic clothesline won't heat and give better purchase for climbing plants.

Plants that twine or cling are easier to manage than stiff, floppy branches that have to be tied or stapled again and again. Fence plantings take more grooming than other plants; usually take monthly trimming to keep them from running wild. Furthermore, if you

plan to repaint your fence, you'll have to take the vines down from time to time; training them on wires makes this operation easier.

Your nurseryman will have some good suggestions for specific plants. Tops on any list are varieties of roses, clematis, wisteria, honeysuckle, and ivy, though even these will not grow in certain areas. A variety of annuals, also, may be trained to give a spot of color which can be changed from year to year. Among these are sweet peas, nasturtiums, morning glory, and for leaves, variegated hop. For more specific and unusual ideas see the *Sunset* book *Landscaping for Western Living.*

John Robinson, Photo

Clematis armandii grows rapidly, keeps leaves year around, flowers in spring. Vine is held on the fence with staples

Clyde Childress, Photo

Ivy screen is 9 feet high. These vines were started on 4-foot mesh fence, supported on framework of wires above that

Art Hupy, Photo

In a rural setting you can change lines of a rail fence near house by letting vines twine along rails between the posts

Clyde Childress, Photo

Wire mesh fence designed to keep dogs at bay is softened by planting of yellow marguerite. Fence pushes color streetward

Virginia Davidson, Design and Photo

Sand castings of lightweight aggregate make interesting free form fence. They look well mounted against solid panel

Eckbo, Royston & Williams, Design; William Aplin, Photo

Cut-out forms of painted plywood decorate steel chain link fence. The designs are fastened against fence with bolts

FENCE DECORATION . . . color, design, lighting

A fence, particularly when it serves as the wall of an outdoor room, lends itself to a number of decorative possibilities. The decoration adds color, interest, and makes the fence seem more like a room wall. When a fence serves as a distant wall for an indoor room, some whimsical notes on the panels will help to break up the penned-in feeling.

There are some noticeable differences between decorating outdoor and indoor areas. A picture, for instance, that is the right size for an indoor wall may look like a postage stamp on a fence 60 feet long under the infinite ceiling of the sky. Normally you sit farther away from a fence than from an indoor wall, so your outdoor decorative scale should be larger.

Weathering is another consideration. For permanence you must select materials that will take extremes of sun, wind, rain, and temperature change. This doesn't mean the materials must be indestructible. You may want to change the scheme after a year or two. Remember, too, that weathering can be an advantage. Wood, copper, brass, bronze, and brick become more beautiful

Virginia Davidson, Design; Ernest Braun, Photo

A mosaic lion adds colorful note to solid panel fence. When plant grows larger, lion will peer out through the "jungle"

(89)

Clyde Childress, Photo
A wicker basket over light bulb throws a striking shadow on fence. If the bulb shows at side, use a tighter weave

Matt Kahn, Design; Ernest Braun, Photo
Above left: A gay and colorful fence mural fits the mood of pool area, relieves march of board that confines swimmers

Matt Kahn, Design
Center: Decorative fence panels are made of welded wrought iron rods which are painted. The circles are harness rings

Douglas Baylis, Design
Below left: For a party effect, candles are mounted on nails. To protect fence, keep candles burning, cover with lanterns

as they weather.

There's no limit to outdoor materials—metal, plastic, concrete, tile, and wood, either carved or in its natural form, are some of your possibilities. Hang them on a fence panel or set them in the structure directly. You might use panels as a backdrop for your own art gallery. If you feel your artistic talent is limited, a local landscape architect or art school may assist you.

Fences are also a powerful element in a garden night lighting scheme. Use them to mount electrical fixtures or to hide reflectors and lamps. A fence is a natural background for a silhouetted plant, and the shadow patterns of branches and leaves against a panel add a new dimension to your garden design. A soft glow of light diffused through a plastic panel is another exciting way to achieve night effects. For temporary decorative needs, such as a party, your fence is one of the few permanent parts of your garden that you can dress up or alter without damage.

WIND TESTS . . . which fence is best?

To get an accurate measure of the difference in comfort obtainable with different fence designs, the editors of *Sunset Magazine* called upon engineers at the University of California to test the effectiveness of various types of fences in warding off wind.

What the engineers measured was the effect of the fences on *comfort temperature*—the temperature you *feel*. Comfort temperature is a complex measurement that combines into a single reading all the factors that affect your well being—temperature of the air, velocity of the wind, relative humidity, etc.

The engineers made the tests outdoors with full-sized fence panels and in a wind tunnel with scale models. They first took a reading of the comfort temperature in the direct path of the wind, then they placed the test fences across the wind and took comparative readings to determine how much difference the fence made. The more efficient the fence as a wind screen, the more it raised the comfort temperature.

The results of these tests are shown in the charts that follow. Degree marks at each 2-foot interval indicate how much higher the comfort temperature was at that spot with the fence in place than it was without this protection.

SOLID FENCE

Wind washes over a solid fence in much the same way water would wash over a solid, straight up-and-down barrier thrust into a fast running stream.

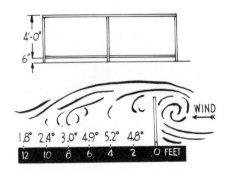

The tests showed that this results in a somewhat lower comfort temperature near the fence where some of the wind crashes down in a wave-like action.

Maximum protection comes at a distance about equal to the height of the fence, and after this, the protection drops off rather rapidly.

SOLID FENCE PLUS WIND BAFFLE

When a baffle was added to the solid fence, the area of protection was increased considerably. Slanted away from the wind, the baffle lets the wind flow over in a gentle arc—and eliminates the downward crash of wind which comes with a straight up and down solid fence.

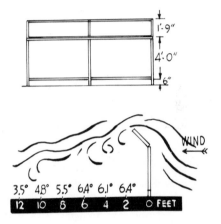

Maximum protection from the baffle fence is reached at a distance equal to slightly more than the height of the fence.

Beyond this, the drop is gradual—so that effective protection extends to more than twice the height of the fence. Tests were also made with the baffle at angles other than 45 degrees. Greatest protection two feet away from the fence came with the baffle at an angle of 65 degrees.

When the baffle is slanted toward the wind, the flow is forced straight up—so that the wind acts

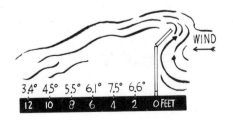

as a partial barrier to itself. This is the type of wind barrier used on board ship to give protection to the bridge.

The tests showed that this type of fence gives greater protection to the area near the fence than any other type tested.

The protection beyond a distance equal to the height of the fence was about the same as for the fence with the baffle away from the wind.

LOUVER FENCE

The louver fence lets some of the wind flow through it—ventilating and protecting at the same time.

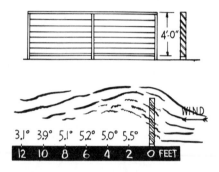

Even with some of the wind flowing through, however, the fence provides a protected area that extends a distance equal to twice the height of the fence.

The increase in comfort temperature was not as great as for either the solid fence or the fence with the baffle, but it gave more stabilized protection over a wider area. Beyond the eight-foot point, the drop was gradual.

When the louver fence was turned around so that the louvers directed the wind down, the protection afforded was considerably less. The louvers bounced

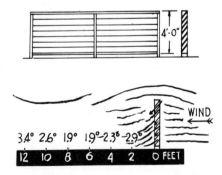

the wind right into the area to be protected. Greatest protection was recorded at 12 feet, at which point the wind apparently was on the rebound to

the extent that a small area was given some very limited protection.

SLAT FENCE

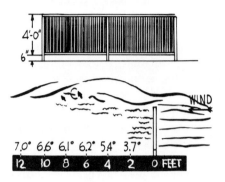

The fence with vertical laths, spaced about ½-inch apart, gave the most unexpected results. The lowest reading for the slat fence was close to the fence, the highest was 12 feet away—a distance equal to three times the height of the fence.

These results may be explained this way: the laths diffuse the wind—let some through, let some over the top. The wind that goes through the screen-like openings between the slats comes out on the other side with a jet-like speed which dissipates most of the wind's energy in the first foot or so. From there on, it forms a layer of slow-moving air that acts as a ceiling to the protected area and prevents the fast-moving air, which rides over the top of the fence, from coming down into the protected area.

CONCLUSIONS

The fence tests, while they didn't prove conclusively that any one fence was a standout better fence than all others under every condition, did prove these things:

1. *The old stand-by, the solid fence, is usually not the best for wind control.*

2. *A screen-like fence, such as the slat fence, can be counted on to protect a wider area than its openness would suggest possible.*

3. *While the fence with the louvers directed to force the wind down is not an effective wind control, it might be used to catch summertime breezes. The results achieved with the louver fence in both positions suggest that a fence with movable louvers might offer interesting possibilities—how much protection you received would depend upon the position of the louvers.*

WHO BUILDS IT? ... you, your neighbor, a contractor?

When you have decided on the kind and location of your garden fence, your next great decision is whether to attempt to build it yourself, have it partly constructed by a contractor, or to pass the entire job along to the professional.

Having the fence built in its entirety by a contractor is certain to cost you more than if you did the job yourself, but there are persuasive reasons for calling him in for the work.

A fence contractor can put a fence in place much more rapidly than the week-end carpenter. The builder has access to specialized fence materials, preservatives, equipment, and experienced labor—a four-star combination that should produce sound results. If you choose a reputable builder, you can have confidence that the fence will be properly built and that if construction defects happen to show up later, you can be reasonably certain that the contractor will correct them.

If you do arrange to have the work done for you, protect yourself (and the contractor) with a written contract. The agreement should specify grades of lumber used, types of preservative, if any, and other important details.

On the other hand, you may have equally persuasive reasons for attempting the task yourself. If you have just purchased your home, you may be enduring the frugal streak that so many home buyers pass through the first few months after closing the deal and paying off all the quaint and unexpected charges that turn up with the final bill. Or perhaps you simply want to create and build some part of your house, to feel that you have had at least a small part in making the new house a home.

If you have a feeling for tools and a capacity for doing reasonably careful work, you should be able to erect a fence that is as sturdy and attractive as a professional job. Fence building is not one of the most difficult forms of carpentry. Materials are usually easy to obtain. Standard lengths of standard lumber can be used to build many types of fences, and materials for fences that require special trim or off-sizes can often be bought pre-cut from lumber yards, mills, or fence dealers. Application of wood preservatives, which was once a messy and tedious task, has been simplified in recent years by the introduction of preservatives that can be applied successfully by soaking.

The only really tough part of building a fence is digging the post holes and setting the posts so they are firmly embedded and precisely aligned. A day spent twisting a post hole auger through unyielding soil can sometimes leave your back muscles feeling as if you had flown a good hundred miles under your own power. If you want to save your back for other garden chores, you may be able to arrange for a mechanical post hole digger to bore the holes, a service that is available in some localities for a small charge per hole.

The task of fitting the posts into the holes so they are in line and will stay in line is an operation that often deters the amateur. Actually, this critical job is easily done if you follow accepted methods; but if you don't trust your skill, you may also be able to hire a fence contractor to set them for you. Many contractors will dig the holes and set the posts for a fee per post. Once your posts are stanchly set, you can attach the rails and pickets or boards with little difficulty.

If your plan calls for a painted fence, you can usually save yourself a tidy sum by wielding the paint brush yourself. The cost of having some types of fences painted often equals the cost of the fence itself.

CHECK LOCAL ORDINANCES

If your fence is to be built outside an incorporated area, you may not have to worry about building restrictions; but if you are building within a city, you had better check with your City Hall.

Most municipalities require a building permit before you can start. In most cities, the local ordinances restrict the height of boundary fences to 6 feet and front yard fences to 3 or 4 feet. Most cities also specify how close to the sidewalk or the street you can build a fence. If your house is located on a corner, you may find that special restrictions apply to fencing the front of your lot. Height of corner fences is often prescribed low enough to permit approaching motorists to see each other before they reach the intersection.

Some cities go further into the matter. Some specify the kinds of materials that can be used within fire zones, some establish specifications for post preservatives, depth of post embedding, and structural provisions for resisting wind pressure.

FENCE LAYOUT... planning avoids problems

Before you get very far into your fence-building project, you should draw up a rough plan of the layout. It need not be very fancy or exact, but it will help you in estimating how much materials you will need and in figuring your way around any problems that you may have to solve along your fence line.

If every lot were as smooth as a baseball diamond, laying out a fence over its surface would be simple indeed. But many lots are not so conveniently planed out. Often, the fence planner has to figure how to get his fence up a steep slope, across a stream, through a large tree. Problems such as these usually call for professional solution, but here are some suggestions that may be helpful.

Trees—Once in a while, the erection of a fence is complicated by one or more trees growing right on the line where the fence should go. If the tree is small and indifferent, it can be taken out if it doesn't fit into the garden plan; but if it is a large, handsome specimen that you want to preserve, you can bring the fence right up to it and stop an inch

or two short of the trunk. Don't place the last post so close to the tree that you will injure the root system when you dig the post hole. The fence should also be designed so that its edge next to the tree can be "pruned" occasionally to accommodate the slow changes in the contour of the trunk.

Don't plan to include the tree in your fence line as a post. It can be done, but the practice is not to be encouraged. A tree is not likely to rupture the fence, for there is actually very little movement in the trunk of a large tree, even under severe wind stress. It will twist like a corkscrew, but it will not sway. Chief hazard in using the tree for a post is the possible injury that may be done to it. If you must attach anything to the trunk, be sparing in the use of nails. They do not of themselves poison the tree, but they break the outer skin of the trunk and

permit disease and bacteria to enter. If too many nails are embedded in the bark or if wire mesh tends to restrict it or girdle it, the tree's sap flow may be stopped, with consequent injury or death. If lumber must be attached to the trunk, fasten it so it is held away from the bark and does not flatten it.

Streams—Where fences cross ditches, streams, or dry washes that flood in winter, much ingenuity is often required to provide fence protection at that point without creating a barrier that will become choked with debris and either cause a neighborhood flood or carry away the fence.

One way to solve the problem is to install a floodgate. These are simple, rugged devices that open automatically at floodstage. A typical gate, as shown in the drawing, pivots on anchor posts on each side of the stream and swings upward as the water rises. Such a gate can also be slung on cables. Two vital requirements for sound design are strong anchor posts on each bank and provisions to prevent erosion of the bank, such as concrete side walls or a matte of saplings or wire. Gates should be cleaned out after every passage of flood water.

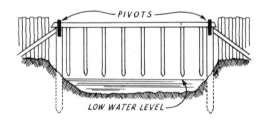

Design of floodgates is best entrusted to an engineer or landscape architect.

Edges of banks—When the fence has to be built along the edge of a stream or bluff, the fence layout should be worked out with an engineer or landscape architect as they will know just how close to the edge the fence can be put without losing it eventually to wind or water action. Often, plantings along the bank will slow down the soil movement.

Rounding a curve—If your fence plan calls for a curve, you can only secure a true arc by using some variety of railless fence, such as woven sapling or driven grapestake. A slat fence can be built so it looks as if it were curved by bringing it around in a series of short chords. A curve in a wire fence under tension presents serious problems (see chapter on wire fencing).

Hillside slope—If your fence line runs up hill, there are two accepted ways to lay out the fence: it may be built to follow the natural contours of the land or it may be brought downhill in steps. Some types of

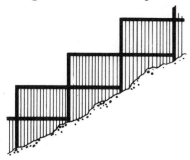

fencing adapt themselves easily to hillside contours, notably post-and-rail, and either rustic or milled pickets.

Less flexible are the more geometric forms, such as solid board, plywood, louver. These can be canted to fit a hillside, but they require very careful cutting and fitting, and they look best if used in stepped sequence. Some suggested ways of using hillside fencing are shown in the drawings.

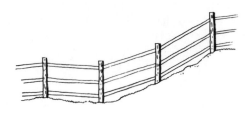

In laying out your fence, you will find it convenient to know exactly how steep the rise may be. There are many ways of determining this, but you can get a reasonably accurate idea by using a line level and a stretch of chalk line. Run the string from a stake at the high point in your fence line. Tie the

string to the stake at ground level, and stretch it to a tall stake at the lowest point. Draw the string taut, hang the line level on the *center* of the string, and shift the string up or down on the tall stake as necessary until the bubble is centered. To be sure of an accurate reading, make certain that the twine does not touch anything—even blades of grass—and take measurements on a windless day. To calculate the drop, divide the height of the string above grade on the tall stake into the length of line between stakes.

WHERE TO GET HELP

In cases where you have a difficult engineering problem, or want advice on specific ways to fit your fencing program into an overall landscape design, you may want to call on professional help. The cost of such aid will vary according to the quality of the designer and how much planning assistance you require.

The most complete and integrated solution is to hire a landscape architect to plan your entire garden. He works much the same way as any other architect, submitting preliminary plans, and when one is approved he supplies finished drawings and a planting list. Depending upon your agreement, he may also supervise the actual construction. Fees usually are based on a percentage of the complete installation costs.

Sometimes you can work with a landscape architect on a consultation basis, paying him by the hour. Under this arrangement he would help you with preliminary planning, then visit a couple of times during the installation process. Or you might work out a partial plan agreement whereby he designs and supplies plans for just the fencing at a specified fee.

A fence contractor is also often prepared to offer you low cost design service, usually with the stipulation that you buy your materials from him, and let him do a part of the installation. Of course, if you hire a contractor to do the entire job, you have the benefit of his engineering experience, and a reasonable assurance that he will install the fence to last, as well as correct any defects in construction.

Whether you choose a landscape architect or a contractor, it's a good idea to examine some of his previous work and talk with some of his former clients before you sign a contract. Don't be influenced by price alone —a poor job is no bargain at any price.

Highly paid professionals are not your only sources for design help. A city building inspector or county agent can usually tell you if your fence engineering is feasible, and often solves a few of your knotty problems in the course of a routine inspection. Don't expect these officials to provide free landscaping designs, however, that's not part of their job.

BUILDING MATERIALS . . . quality affects fence lifespan

A garden fence is not expected to last for generations, but if it is built of good quality materials that are weather- and decay-resistant, it should last for 15 to 20 years, possibly longer. The difference between using poor quality and good quality materials can often mean a difference of 15 years in the life expectancy of a fence.

Actually, the material costs of a fence are so much less than the cost of labor that there is little value to be gained in scrimping. An extra $2.00 spent on nails, for example, can add years to the attractive life of a fence.

The chief material requirement is for lumber—and plenty of it. Secondary needs are nails, paint, preservatives.

LUMBER

Some types of fences can be built from logs and saplings cut on the site, but most fence builders rely on the dressed lumber obtainable in the lumber yard or the prefabricated fencing available in many localities.

If pre-built fencing is obtainable in your area, you can save yourself all the bother of estimating, ordering, and cutting lumber to fit your plans.

Package fences usually include all the materials needed for the complete installation, down to the last nail. The fence kits provide posts that have been treated, cut to proper length, and notched or mortised as necessary to accommodate the rails; rails that have been cut to exact length for uniform span between posts and trimmed as necessary to fit into the posts; and shaped pickets, bound in bundles or in rolls, woven together with copper or galvanized wire. Surprisingly, even rough-and-ready fencing like post-and-rail is obtainable from the fence factory, and once it is put together it looks as if it had been hewn and fitted on the spot.

Pre-built fence materials are usually sold by the running foot or by the panel. They are retailed through lumber dealers, garden stores, and fence contractors. They can also be bought from mail order houses or direct from the factory.

GRADES OF LUMBER

Whether the lumber is bought in a fence kit or direct from the lumber dealer, it should conform to certain standards.

Construction lumber is sold in a variety of grades. Best quality is smoothly finished and generally free of knots and blemishes. Unless the appearance of the wood itself is vital to the fence design, there is nothing to be gained by buying the topmost grades at what may amount to three times the price you would have to pay for lesser grades that are thoroughly satisfactory for fence construction. The knots and other defects that make lumber unsuitable for finishing work, do not interfere with the usefulness of a fence, particularly if the surface is painted.

Lumber used should be reasonably dry and seasoned, although in some types of fences, raw, green lumber can be used quite successfully.

For many types, rough-finished lumber is adequate. It is heavier and cheaper than finished lumber, but it is harder to paint and its dimensions are likely to be irregular. Lumber that is finished on one edge or side is often satisfactory.

VARIETIES OF LUMBER

Some varieties of wood are regarded as particularly suited to fence building because they are naturally resistant to decay. Lumber cut from the heart of redwood, cedar, or cypress logs is strongly rot-resistant. However, lumber cut from areas close to the bark of these trees will rot out almost as quickly as lumber from decay-susceptible woods like pine and fir.

Although entire fences are commonly built of decay-resistant wood, the principal need for this immunity is in the posts which are vulnerable to attack by fungi and wood-destroying insects. Other parts of the fence, such as the rails, pickets, and boards, are exposed to sunlight and air and do not succumb so quickly to decay. It is therefore not uncommon to use heartwood for the posts and sapwood for the remainder of the structure; or to use redwood or cedar for the posts and some other variety of wood, such as pine or fir, for the other parts. Under ordinary circumstances, the decay-susceptible woods are satisfactory for the exposed, upper portions of the fence, particularly if the fence is to be painted.

It is not always possible to obtain redwood, cedar, or cypress in sufficient quantity for a long fence line, or even for the two dozen posts needed for the average lot. Fortunately, other varieties of lumber can be made decay-resistant by proper application of wood preservatives (see below). For example, a pine post, which will normally rot out in 3 to 5 years, can be made to last 15 to 20 years by impregnating it with preservative. A pressure-treated, creosoted post is likely to stand for 35 years.

Redwood, cedar, and other decay-resistant woods can be treated with preservatives, but the value of such treatment is open to debate. The heartwood of these varieties is so dense that it will absorb little or none of the solution. Sapwood will absorb it more readily, but the use of sapwood in the fence then offers no advantages over other varieties of wood, which may be cheaper and more easily obtained.

LUMBER SIZES

Lumber used in fence building is drawn from stock sizes. Here are the recommended dimensions:

Posts—Should be 2 to 2½ feet longer than the height of the fence, thus, a 6-foot fence would require an 8- to 8½-foot post. High, solid board fences need extra long posts to permit a deeper foundation; figure the length as 40% longer than height of fence.

Use 4"x4" or doubled 2"x4" posts for solid fences not over 4 feet high, or picket-type fences not over 6 feet. Also suitable for wire fences and lightweight rail fences.

Use 6"x6" posts for gate and corner posts in 3- to 4-foot fences; as line posts for solid 6-foot fences; or when rails of a lightweight fence are mortised into post.

Use 8"x8" posts as gate and corner posts for solid 6-foot fences; as line posts for solid fences subject to heavy wind pressure; and as support posts for overhead structures attached to the fence, such as egg-crate or lattice roof.

Round posts, made from peeled logs, should be slightly larger than squared posts. In place of 4"x4" milled post, substitute peeled post 6 inches in diameter at butt end. For 6"x6", substitute 8-inch diameter; for 8"x8", 10-inch.

Standard distance between posts is 8 feet for picket and board fences; 10 feet for rail fences.

Rails—Rails can be 12, 16, or 18 feet in length, but they should not be attached unsupported for spans longer than 9 feet. Thus, an 18-foot rail should be supported by a center post to reduce the span to the recommended distance.

Use 2"x4" for most purposes: top and bottom rails for picket, slat, or board fences. For heavier fence, use 3"x4"; for lightweight palings, you can use 2"x3"; as a light rail, you can even use 1"x4".

Pickets—Milled pickets are obtainable in a wide range of sizes. Widths run from 1¼ to 5½ inches; lengths, from 2 to 5 feet; thickness is usually 1 inch. Most popular size: 3"x36".

Rustic pickets, such as grape stakes and cedar saplings, average about 2 inches in width, and range in height from 3 to 8 feet. Cedar palings are obtainable woven together in panels 3 to 5 feet in width or in rolls from 8 to 10 feet in length.

Utility fencing, composed of 4-foot lath pickets woven in wire, is obtainable in 50- to 100-foot rolls. It can be bought in red, green, white, or natural.

Boards — For solid-surfaced fences, 1x8's and 1x10's are usually used, whether nailed on vertically or horizontally. For post and board fences, popular sizes are 1x6 and 1x8; 1x4's are also used with some lighter fences.

For tight surfacing, tongue-and-groove or shiplap siding is required. *Caution:* Be sure to allow for expansion and contraction of the wood when using interlocking lumber, remember to set joints loose.

COSTS OF LUMBER

The cost of lumber used in fencing varies with the ups and downs in general building costs. Wooden fences are not cheap. The board footage of lumber required in, say, 100 feet of fencing is surprisingly large, even with widely spaced pickets. Cost of materials used in post and rail fences usually totals about 25 per cent less than in picket type fences.

NAILS

An important detail that assures long life and clean appearance for a fence is the use of proper type nails. Under some conditions, any kind of nail will do, but for maximum protection against staining and rusting, the nails specially developed for outdoor use are best

Of the outdoor nails, the galvanized is probably the most popular. It is a tough nail, being simply a standard steel nail plated with a thick coating of zinc. It will withstand weathering for many years, although the protective film of zinc does leach off in time, exposing the steel core to rust. In most localities, this action takes a long time; but in areas subject to corrosive winds, as along the seashore or near some industrial plants, galvanized nails may rust out in a relatively short time.

Probably the most suitable nails, though not always the most easily obtained, are those made of aluminum alloy. They "rust" like any other metal, but the action is slow, almost imperceptible, and they do not stain wood or paint. They are not as hard as galvanized nails and tend to bend if driven into hard wood, such as fir, but they are rugged enough for redwood, cedar, and other soft woods commonly used for fencing. They are more expensive than galvanized nails, but the few dollars extra cost is a small item in the fence budget, and may be repaid later through savings in repainting costs.

Steel nails are least satisfactory, although they may be used if they are thoroughly and constantly protected from the weather by paint. They are thus suited to types of fences that must be kept well painted, such as the familiar white picket or rail fences. Blued steel and cement-coated nails are slightly more rust-resistant than uncoated nails. The cement coating provides a tighter nailing job temporarily, but the cement will dissolve in time and lose its grip on wood and steel.

STANDARD DIMENSIONS OF SURFACED LUMBER

THICKNESS		WIDTH		SQUARES	
Rough	Surfaced	Rough	Surfaced	Rough	Surfaced
1"	$^{25}/_{32}$"	3"	$2\frac{5}{8}$"	3x3	$2\frac{5}{8}$ x $2\frac{5}{8}$
$1\frac{1}{4}$"	1-$\frac{1}{16}$"	4"	$3\frac{5}{8}$"	4x4	$3\frac{5}{8}$ x $3\frac{5}{8}$
$1\frac{1}{2}$"	1-$\frac{5}{16}$"	5"	$4\frac{5}{8}$"	5x5	$4\frac{5}{8}$ x $4\frac{5}{8}$
2"	1-$\frac{3}{4}$"	6"	$5\frac{5}{8}$"	6x6	$5\frac{5}{8}$ x $5\frac{5}{8}$
3"	2-$\frac{5}{8}$"	8"	$7\frac{1}{2}$"	8x8	$7\frac{1}{2}$ x $7\frac{1}{2}$
4"	3-$\frac{5}{8}$"	10"	$9\frac{1}{2}$"		
		12"	$11\frac{1}{2}$"		

TABLE FOR CONVERTING LINEAL TO BOARD FEET

LUMBER SIZE	LINEAL FEET								
	8	10	12	14	16	18	20	22	24
1x2	Sold by lineal foot								
1x3	Sold by lineal foot								
1x4	2-⅔	3-⅓	4	4-⅔	5-⅓	6	6-⅔	7-⅓	8
1x6	4	5	6	7	8	9	10	11	12
1x8	5-⅓	6-⅔	8	9-⅓	10-⅔	12	13-⅓	14-⅔	16
1x10	6-⅔	8-⅓	10	11-⅔	13-⅓	15	16-⅔	18-⅓	20
1x12	8	10	12	14	16	18	20	22	24
2x2	Sold by lineal foot								
2x3	Sold by lineal foot								
2x4	5-⅓	6-⅔	8	9-⅓	10-⅔	12	13-⅓	14-⅔	16
2x6	8	10	12	14	16	18	20	22	24
2x8	10-⅔	13-⅓	16	18-⅔	21-⅓	24	26-⅔	29-⅓	32
2x10	13-⅓	16-⅔	20	23-⅓	26-⅔	30	33-⅓	36-⅔	40
2x12	16	20	24	28	32	36	40	44	48
3x6	12	15	18	21	24	27	30	33	36
4x4	10-⅔	13-⅓	16	18-⅔	21-⅓	24	26-⅔	29-⅓	32

Formula for computing board feet: Thickness in inches x width in feet x length in feet.
Example: 1"x1"x10' = 1x1/12x10 = $\frac{10}{12}$ = 5/6 board foot.

PRESERVATIVES . . . protect posts against decay

Decay is the natural enemy of the garden fence. It is most likely to develop at points where the fence structure touches or enters the ground, wherever two pieces of wood fit tightly together, on surfaces where moisture can collect, or in joints between wood framing and other construction materials.

The decay that shortens the life of a fence is caused by fungus growth. Whenever fungus spores, always present in the air and the soil, find a comfortable environment in a fence post or joint, they settle back and give off a substance that literally dissolves the wood fibers, converting it to foodstuff for themselves. This process can be prevented or thwarted in various ways.

Some kinds of wood protect themselves against fungus invasion. Their fibers contain phenol substances that are either toxic to the fungi or break up the wood-dissolving agent that the fungi produce. Redwood, cedar, cypress, locust, and other woods noted for their durability, resist decay in this manner.

Exposed surfaces can be coated with a good quality paint, which provides a protective skin that fungus spores cannot penetrate, but if this seal is broken at any point, or sloughed off, the spores get under the paint and go to work on the wood as enthusiastically as on unpainted wood. Paint has no protective value whatsoever under ground.

Some kinds of wood that are not naturally resistant to fungus infestation can be provided with artificial immunity by chemical means. Wood preservatives, either soaked or forced into the wood fibers, will create a hostile environment for wood-destroying fungi and insects. Modern preservatives can make non-resistant woods, such as pine, cottonwood, aspen last as long as the more renowned redwood and cypress.

To give full protection, chemical preservatives must be applied so they saturate the fibers of the wood. Thick, viscous preservatives, like creosote, must be forced into the wood under pressure to insure adequate penetration; other more volatile kinds, such as pentachlorophenol and copper naphthenate, can be introduced by prolonged soaking of the wood in a bath of the solution. For that matter, these preservatives are reasonably effective if brushed or sprayed on surfaces that are not subject to severe conditions.

CREOSOTE

Creosote is the granddaddy of the post preservatives. It has been successfully used for decades to protect telegraph poles, railroad ties, and line fence posts.

Although it is a very effective preservative if properly applied, it has some unpleasant traits that make it unpopular with many fence builders. Principal objection is that once a post has been treated, the dressed area can never be painted over, for the brown stain will quickly come through the paint. Many people also object to its heavy, medicinal odor. However, the overpowering odor and the staining effects may not be a disadvantage in some fence installations, such as a wire fence in the country, or a rustic, unpainted fence in the city.

For utmost effectiveness, creosote should be applied under pressure, as it does not readily penetrate the fibers of wood. Such a procedure is well beyond the capacity of the homeowner, since it demands large and expensive equipment; but the process is done commercially, and pressure-treated fence posts are obtainable from some dealers.

For the homeowner, the most practical method of applying creosote is to soak it into the post. This will not give the extra long life that pressure-treating will, but a properly soaked post will last for a good many years. Posts treated in this fashion are also obtainable from dealers.

Brushing creosote on the surface to be buried in the soil is a waste of time.

PENTACHLOROPHENOL

Pentachlorophenol is one of the most effective and convenient of the preservatives that have been developed in recent years. The appealing quality to the homeowner is that it is clean and odorless. Also, when applied with a clear oil, it leaves no stain.

Pentachlorophenol is obtainable under several trade names. It comes in two forms. One, called a toxic wood preservative, is simply the chemical dissolved in oil. The other, called a toxic *water repellent* wood preservative, has added to it certain resins which make the wood almost completely resistant to water penetration.

After treatment with the water repellent preservative, evaporation from treated areas leaves each tiny wood cell wall lined with a permanent elastic film. As a result of this moisture exclusion, the cracking, swelling, and dimensional changes which normally take place in aging are fairly well controlled.

Recommendations by state colleges and forest laboratories call for at least 5 per cent pentachlorophenol by weight for heavy-duty work. A preparation with less than this simply will not do the job where wood is in direct contact with the soil or close to it. Concentrated solutions (the cheapest way to buy it) are obtainable that contain about 25 per cent pentachlorophenol by weight. These are to be diluted with stove oil, diesel oil, or, in a pinch, crankcase drainings filtered through cheesecloth. Dilution of 1 part concentrate with 4 parts thinner will produce a 5 per cent solution.

Some lumber yards carry lumber that has been treated at the mill. Pressure treatment under controlled conditions is far more effective than any home treatment.

In whatever manner you apply pentachlorophenol, be careful to avoid hitting any of the plants in the garden with it. It has a secondary use as a weed-killer, and it will knock over a broad-leafed plant on contact.

COPPER NAPHTHENATE

Copper naphthenate is another very effective preservative that has entered the market in recent years.

An odorless liquid, it may be applied by dipping, brushing, or even spraying in some instances. One of its strong points is that it is non-corrosive and has no injurious effect on plantings.

Commonly available in green color, it may be used as a green stain. Paint may be applied over it, for the color does not come through paint, but it should not of itself be applied over existing paint or varnish.

This preservative is not soluble in water, hence will not leach out.

ZINC NAPHTHENATE

A new-type preservative designed for use where a green stain would be objectionable. It is colorless, can be used under varnish. Applied by dipping, brushing, or spraying.

ZINC CHLORIDE

Zinc chloride was at one time a favored post preservative, but it has been displaced by more effective solutions. It can be used successfully to replace the sap in some kinds of green posts, such

as white birch, but with other woods its effects are not long lasting. It is soluble in water and eventually leaches out.

HOT TAR

Some fence builders advise dipping the ends of fence posts in molten tar, but forestry researchers caution against the practice. According to these authorities, the tar seal tends to trap moisture in the post and create an ideal environment for decay-producing fungi. Even if the post were perfectly dry when it was coated, it would eventually become damp as it absorbed rain water above the tar base.

A tar collar between the post and a concrete footing is sometimes needed to protect the concrete against swelling of the post in freezing weather. (See below.)

PRECAUTIONS IN HANDLING

Some preservatives can be severely injurious to the skin. Care must be taken to avoid contacting the material or splashing it into the eyes. For this reason, it's a good idea to wear goggles and synthetic rubber gloves while working with the material. Once the treated wood has dried, it does not present any hazard.

The petroleum solvent used in some products is inflammable, so they should not be handled near an open flame.

METHODS FOR TREATING POSTS

The method for treating fence posts is simple and inexpensive. The typical treatment is as follows: Usually only 30 inches of the post is treated, which takes care of the 24 inches below the soil and the 6 inches above. It is most essential to cover this section because both insects and fungi thrive in a moist atmosphere. Ideal conditions for their activi-

ties are found in the top layer of soil where moisture, temperature, and air supply are found in the right combination. That is why posts in the ground rot first just below the soil line. Incidentally, the richer the garden soil, the quicker a post will rot out.

To further insure adequate protection, the surface of the post may be pierced all around at the 24-inch mark, or at whatever point the post contacts the soil level. This pre-soaking incision breaks the outer vertical fibers and allows the preservative solution to soak in even farther. The task is best done with a special implement, called an incising tool, which is simply a single-bit Tennessee axe with two rows of sharp teeth mounted on the back of the head.

Ordinary 50-gallon oil drums can be used as containers for the treating solution. After 24 hours of soaking, a post will have an unbroken ring of

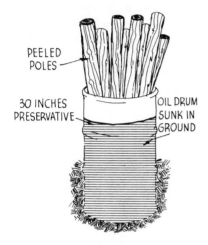

PEELED POLES

30 INCHES PRESERVATIVE

OIL DRUM SUNK IN GROUND

treated wood, penetrating at least one-half to three-quarters of an inch.

Researchers have found that pines can absorb the proper amount of pentachlorophenol for efficient preservation (4 to 5 pounds of preservative to a cubic foot of wood) within 12 to 24 hours. Douglas fir, redwood, incense cedar required a longer period —as long as a week.

The method described above is known as the cold soak method, in contrast to another method used on large scale commercial jobs: the hot-and-cold method, where posts are placed in a hot treating solution which is then cooled, causing the air spaces within the wood to contract and draw the preservative solution up into it. (If you want to try this method yourself, write to University of Wisconsin for Stencil Circular 292, *Longer Service from Fence Posts.*)

TREATING PICKETS AND RAILS

For long fence life, preservative should be used where any wood decay is likely to take place. Wood that is going to be placed within a foot of the ground should be soaked if at all possible. Where soaking is out of the question, paint the wood—literally sop it on—with a paint brush loaded with pre-

servative solution. Pay particular attention to the ends of boards, where entry of moisture is most likely.

The ground stringer should be completely soaked from one end to the other. A long horizontal tub would be the best way to handle this.

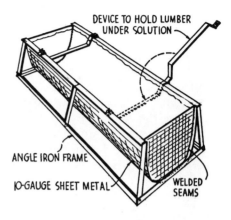

DEVICE TO HOLD LUMBER UNDER SOLUTION

ANGLE IRON FRAME

10-GAUGE SHEET METAL

WELDED SEAMS

The lower 6 inches of vertical boards should be soaked in the same manner as the posts. It would seem that the upper stringer could remain untreated. However, dampness is sure to gather at the ends, where the stringers join the posts. So the

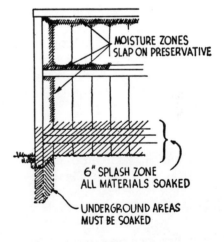

MOISTURE ZONES SLAP ON PRESERVATIVE

6" SPLASH ZONE ALL MATERIALS SOAKED

UNDERGROUND AREAS MUST BE SOAKED

stringer ends, too, should be soaked in the preservative. It would be a good idea to paint *every* joint after the fence is constructed.

Paint the exposed top surfaces of posts, too. This will prevent decay which results from standing water.

In the Northwest, and elsewhere where the year-around atmosphere is moist, it is best to soak completely *all* the wood pieces, for air-borne moisture can do as much damage as underground dampness.

POST HOLES . . . how to stake out, dig

First practical step in building your fence is plotting its exact course and marking the line with stakes and string. If the fence is located on or next to a boundary line, you will find it prudent to have an engineer or surveyor lay out the corner stakes. Although such a survey will cost you a small fee, it will be much less than the later cost of shifting a stanchly built fence.

Of course, if your original survey stakes are still in place marking the boundaries of a newly surveyed lot, you might feel safe in using them for your fence line. Also, if the description of your property is exact enough in your deed, you might be able to measure out the lines yourself. However, if you do so, you would be wise to enlist the cooperation of your interested neighbors to avoid any possible misunderstanding.

Once you have established the end and corner points of your fence, the procedure from there on is simple. You will need a long tape, preferably steel; a carpenter's square; a ball of mason's twine, or any tightly-twisted string, such as discarded fishing line; some stakes; a hatchet; and a piece of colored chalk.

Here's the order of business:

1. Mark the end or corner points with a solidly driven stake, if each point is not already staked.
2. Run mason's twine between the stakes, draw it tight, and tie it firmly to the stakes. If bushes or other obstructions are in the way, use tall stakes so the twine will clear them.
3. Locate the sites for the remaining posts and mark them with stakes. There are several ways to do this. You can simply lay the rails in line along the ground between the end stakes and drive in a stake wherever they butt against each other; or you can measure the intervals with your tape, either laying it along the ground or measuring along the stretched twine. If you do the latter, make provision for variations in distance between posts due to sloping ground. Posts come closer together on slanting ground than on flat.

HOW TO CHECK A RIGHT-ANGLE

If your fence has a right-angle turn, lay out the corner with a carpenter's square. You can check it with a simple trick known as the "three-four-five" rule. Here's how it works:

1. On one of the corner lines, measure off 3 feet from the corner post and mark the string at that point with colored chalk.
2. On the other string, presumably at a right angle, measure off 4 feet from the corner post and mark the point with chalk.
3. Now measure the distance between the two chalk marks. If the measurement is exactly 5 feet, your angle is correct. If it is more, or less, your fence lines are off, and you should shift them until the two points come out at 5 feet.

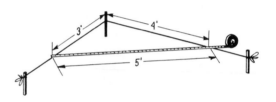

You can apply this rule with greater accuracy by increasing the size of the triangle, using multiples of 3, 4, and 5 feet. For example, points marked on one line at 9 feet and 12 feet on the other would check out with a third measurement of 15 feet; with a multiple of 4, the three figures would be 12, 16, and 20 feet.

DIGGING POST HOLES

When your fence line is strung and the post hole sites staked out, you are ready to start digging.

The proper-sized hole to dig depends on the kind of soil on which your fence is being built. The hole should be of a size that will give firm support to the post and at the same time permit water to drain away from around it.

In open, sandy soils, make the hole only slightly bigger than the post. In heavy clay or adobe, make the hole much larger and pack with gravel. The gravel packing encourages water to drain away instead of remaining trapped around the post. If posts are to be set in concrete, excavate 2½ to 3 times the diameter of the post.

Usually the fence dealer or lumber yard that sold you your posts will lend you a digger; or if you prefer to pass the work along to a machine, you can probably arrange to have the holes dug by an expert with a specially-rigged jeep.

If you plan to buy a post hole digger, you will find several types from which to choose, and you should try to buy the variety that will bite into your own peculiar soil.

If your soil is free of rocks, you will find the post hole auger to be the quickest tool to use. This is an implement tipped with a screw blade on the business end and fixed with a wooden crossbar on the other for you to twist for motive power. There are two types on the market: one is simply a large twist drill, the other has cutting blades combined with a scoop arrangement that holds the loose soil as it is bored out and also discourages the wall of the hole from caving in. Either type is satisfactory. They are obtainable in a choice of 6- or 8-inch blade diameters.

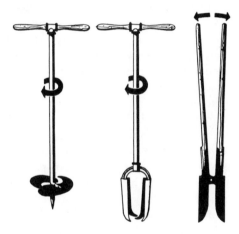

An auger will not perform to advantage in rocky soil. Here you will need a two-handled, clam-shell digger. The fence builder plunges the blades into the soil and by working the handles back and forth chews his way into the soil. This type of digger is difficult to use after the hole gets down to 2 feet or so, because the side walls interfere with spreading the handles apart. Working the handles back and forth also tends to break down the walls and to produce a cavernous hole, larger and more ragged than the neatly drilled bore that an auger can produce.

In very rocky soil, a digging bar and a spoon-bladed shovel may be the only combination that will work—aside from dynamite.

COPING WITH ROCK

Unfortunately, the rigid need for even spacing of posts on 8- or 10-foot centers often forces the builder to plant a post in a spot occupied by a rock. If the stone is not too large, it can often be broken up in the soil and removed piecemeal. A substantial crowbar will break up a soft stone, but a tough one will need special tools. Stonemasons drill a hole with a star drill and insert special wedges known as "feathers." A few blows with a sledge on the wedge will usually crack the stone.

If the stone turns out to be a giant boulder of unguessed subterranean dimensions, it is best left unremoved, and the fence post should be attached to it by means of a steel pin. Drill into the stone

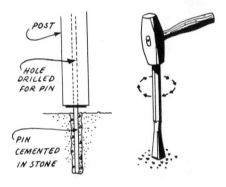

with a 1-inch star drill to a depth of 4-6 inches. (To use a star drill, turn it around slowly and steadily and at the same time strike it with a heavy hammer.) Drill a ¾-inch hole in the base of the post to a depth of a foot. As this hole must be precisely centered and exactly true, it should be drilled on a lathe or in a shop. Insert a ¾-inch steel rod into the post and set it in hole in the stone. True up the post, brace it, and pour thin concrete paste into the hole, filling in around the pin. Keep damp and let cure 48 hours.

ERECTING THE FENCE ... how to go about it

When you have finished digging the post holes, you are ready to move on to the next phase, the real business of putting the fence together. The assembling sequence will vary according to the type of fence under construction or the personal preferences of the builder himself.

Basically, there are three accepted ways for putting up the fence.

Some builders prefer to set all the posts in place and attach the other parts later. This procedure is usually followed for wire fences, woven pickets, and other types with butted rail joints. Posts are also erected in a single step when they are anchored in concrete, because work on the rest of the fence must be held back until the concrete has cured.

As another variation, posts and rails can be put up at the same time. This is practiced, of course, with post-and-rail fences, but it is also used with other types of fences when the rails and posts must be fitted together with some kind of interlocking joint. If rails are to be joined in this manner to concrete-anchored posts, it is important to attach them before the concrete hardens.

Some builders prefer to assemble the fence in sections, filling in the rails and pickets whenever two line posts are in place. This method has the advantage of strengthening the fence structure as it grows, and it prevents the rails from sagging. Some types of fences, such as louver, board, and panel-picket, can be built in sections formed and nailed together flat on the ground, then lifted into place, and attached to the posts.

SETTING THE POSTS

Setting the posts is the most critical stage in fence building. A good looking fence that runs straight and true relies upon carefully set posts for its clean, disciplined lines. Posts must be solidly embedded so they will not lean with the weight of the fence, and they must be plumb and accurately aligned.

You will need all or some of these tools: a carpenter's level, plumb bob, mason's twine, tamping bar (or a 5-foot length of heavy pipe, capped on one end), a heavy hammer, and some 20-penny nails. If your fence posts are to be set in concrete, you will require some additional materials and equipment, as indicated below.

There are three ways of setting the posts firmly

in the ground: they may be held in place by tamped soil or gravel, by cleats nailed to the underground portion of the post, or by a collar of concrete. The method chosen will depend upon soil and drainage conditions and the type and weight of fence struc-

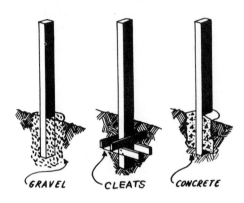

ture. In soil that is reasonably stable, posts may be set in the earth that is dug out for the hole or a gravel packing can be tamped in place. If soil is unstable—likely to sluice away in winter or bulge and crack in summer—a concrete collar or sub-soil cleats are usually indicated. Concrete footings are also recommended for heavy fences or those that must withstand strong winds.

The easiest way to make sure that your fence will follow a straight line is to start off with opposite corner posts. Set one permanently in place and fix the other one securely but not so firmly that it cannot be shifted slightly. Stretch a chalk line tautly between them and start building from the permanently fixed post toward the other one. The chalk line will serve as a guide in lining up the posts as you proceed. When you reach the loosely set corner post, you can make any necessary adjustments in its position and then fix it permanently.

If the fence has a gate, the gate posts should be set in place first and the gate hung. The hinge post is placed first, the gate attached to it, and the opposite post then set permanently in position. Hardware is attached to the post before it is erected.

HOW TO SET THE POSTS PLUMB

First, shovel 3 or 4 inches of gravel into the bottom of the post hole, tamp it down, and then place the post on top of it. Fill in about 6 inches of gravel or soil around the post, tamp it firmly enough to hold the post upright, then true up the post before filling in the remainder of the packing.

If it is a squared post, it can be lined up by either of two tested methods:

1. Check the two sides with a carpenter's level, or
2. Check with a plumb bob. Suspend the bob from a string attached to a nail driven into a *corner* of the post, as shown in the drawing.

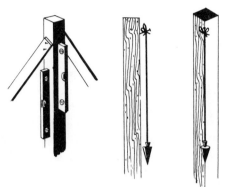

By matching the bob line against the corner line from two directions, you can ascertain if the post is plumb in both directions.

A round field post is harder to check with instruments. If the post is not too irregular in shape, it can be lined up with the level or plumb bob, but often the only way to do it properly is to rely on the human eye—preferably four of them. While the fence builder holds the post erect, his helper should walk some distance away and check its alignment visually from several different points.

Once the post is plumbed, it should be braced to hold it temporarily in position while construction proceeds. Strengthen it with outrigger braces, one end nailed to the post, the other embedded in the soil and bolstered with a stake. Check the post alignment again, then fill in the hole with soil, gravel, or concrete (see below). Tamp the gravel solidly in place. Leave the braces attached until after the rails have been nailed on. The bracing will help the post to resist the shock of nailing.

ANCHORING POSTS IN CONCRETE

Concrete is a mixture of cement, sand, gravel, and water that is bonded together by a chemical reaction between the water and the cement. You can buy it in several forms.

You may obtain cement, sand, and gravel and blend them yourself; or you may get the sand and gravel already mixed, requiring only the addition of cement; or you may buy all three ingredients premixed. The latter is obtainable under various trade names, factory-blended and bagged. With the addition of water, this mix is ready for use. This is a relatively expensive way to buy the dry ingredients; but it is a convenient form to use, because it eliminates the drudgery of blending the ingredients in their dry state.

Estimating amount needed — Concrete is sold by cubic measure. As a rule of thumb, figure on ⅔ cubic foot of poured concrete to each post hole. This will require 1 cubic foot of dry ingredients, as water compacts the mix one-third when it is added to the dry mixture.

The formula recommended for fence post footings is 1 part cement, 3 parts clean sand, and 5 parts gravel with no pebbles larger than ¾ inch. Follow this table for estimating your needs:

		No. Posts		
Separate Ingredients	3	9	18	27
Cement (sacks).............	⅓	1	2	3
Sand (cubic feet)	1	3	6	9
Gravel (cubic feet)........	1⅔	5	10	15
Dry-Mix (sacks).............	3	9	18	27

In some localities, sand and gravel are sold by weight rather than by cubic foot. A cubic foot of sand or gravel weighs between 90 and 120 pounds, depending on how damp it is. Small quantities of sand are often sold by the sack. Each sack of sand (or cement) equals a cubic foot. Allow 5 per cent for wastage.

Mixing—To mix concrete you'll need a pail, and two shovels, one for dry mixing, the other for blending wet. It's neater and more efficient to mix concrete in a metal wheelbarrow or garden cart; you'll need one anyway to move the concrete to your postholes. Some old hands still stick to the mixing board technique, using a tight board or plywood platform. Mixing technique is the same in both cases, but a wheelbarrow eliminates possible water losses.

1. Hand mixing: To prepare concrete from dry ingredients, heap the mixings on the board, one shovelful at a time, keeping the proportions in line with the formula, and blend the ingredients together. To save effort, use the shovel with a rolling motion, turning the ingredients under with the blade. After you have thoroughly blended the dry aggregate and cement, scoop out a hollow in the center of the heap, and fill it partly full of water. Mix in the water by working your way around the edge of the puddle with the shovel, rolling the dry mix into the water with the blade. When mixing on a board, don't break the edge dam or water will escape; with a wheelbarrow the water won't leak out.

If you are working with the separate ingredients, first make a trial batch to test the workability of the formula. The mounds of sand and gravel that you bought are certain to contain enough moisture to

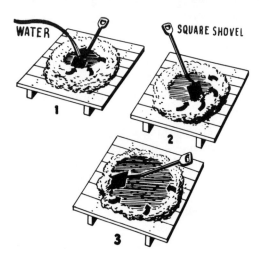

require you to vary the formula slightly. To make the test batch, spread 3 shovelfuls of sand on the mixing board and add 1 shovelful of cement. Blend together until no gray or brown streaks remain. Then spread 5 shovelfuls of gravel over the cement-sand mixture, and blend until the gravel is evenly distributed. Scoop out the center, pour in 3 quarts of water, and mix it in. If the trial batch is too soupy, add a small amount of sand or gravel. If it is too stiff, cut down the quantity of sand or gravel in the next batch.

If you use a prepared dry-mix, you probably won't need to try a test batch. If the mix has been manufactured and marketed under proper conditions, it should reach you in a thoroughly dry state and thus not require any adjustment in the amount of water called for in the instructions printed on the bag. Just empty 2 or 3 sacks on the mixing board, form the heap into volcano-shape, and work in the required amount of water, usually 1 gallon per bag.

2. Machine mixing: Old hands will tell you there is a limit to the amount of concrete that you can comfortably mix at one time on the board or in a boat. If your requirements are for a large volume of concrete, you will save time and sweat by renting a portable mixer and a wheelbarrow. Most efficient mixer for a one or two-man job is the half-bag machine. These are revolved by gasoline or electric motors or by hand. Stay away from the latter: they're not much fun.

Allow the mixture to tumble for 2 or 3 minutes after the water has been added, then pour into a wheelbarrow and dump into the hole.

Setting the Post—To set the post, place it in the hole and shovel in enough gravel to hold it erect, and brace it as outlined above. If the bottom rail of the fence is mortised into the post, fit it in place before pouring the concrete.

Pour the concrete on top of the gravel pad that is holding the post erect. (Don't pour concrete in the bottom of the hole before the post is put in place. This would block drainage.) Fill in the concrete so it forms a collar around the post. Tamp it thoroughly to clear it of air bubbles, distribute the aggregate, and make the mass compact. Bring the concrete a few inches above grade, and finish it off with a smooth sloping cap so it will shed rain water.

Check the straightness of your post as you fill in the concrete. If you have to shift the post to get it back into alignment, do so within a half hour after pouring, otherwise you will weaken the concrete. Leave the post alone for 48 hours. Do not jar it or attempt to nail to it while the concrete is curing.

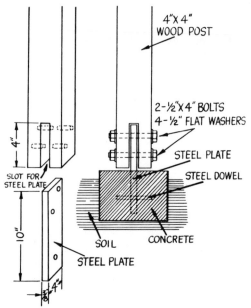

One variation on the standard concrete installation is to embed a steel plate half way into concrete and bolt the post to the free end as in the drawing. If the iron is kept painted this type of installation is long lasting, does away with problem of rotting posts.

Frost Protection—In localities where frost action is severe, it may be necessary to protect the concrete from being ruptured by water freezing in the post.

Rain water soaked up by the post freezes, swells, and cracks the concrete collar. One way to prevent this is to wrap a layer of corrugated cardboard around the post, smooth side out. After the concrete has set, remove the cardboard, melt roofing tar in an old bucket and pour it into the crevice. This will form a flexible collar around the post that will absorb the expansion and contraction of the water-logged post and prevent its damaging the concrete.

CORNER AND GATE POSTS

The point of greatest strain in a fence structure occurs at the corners and at gate posts. In the one case, the pull of the opposing lines of fence (particularly wire mesh) may tend to uproot the post; in the other, the swinging of the gate tends to wiggle it out of plumb.

Ordinarily, the extra strain on corner and gate posts can be absorbed by using a post of a larger size than the line posts and by embedding it 6 to 12 inches deeper. Thus, a fence with 4"x4" posts would require a 6"x6" at the corner or gate, 6"x6" line posts would take an 8"x8". To make certain that the posts will not be swiveled or pulled out of line, you can install anchoring devices, such as the sub-soil cleats. If the post is subject to strong pull, as in a tightly stretched wire fence, elaborate anchoring devices are usually needed (see the chapter on wire fencing). Large, heavy gates, or those that swing across a road, also require substantial bracing (see chapter on gates).

Simplest way to strengthen the installation of a gate or corner post is to attach cross bars ("scabs") to the foot of the post before embedding it. With a narrow gate installation, the scabs can be extended to connect the two posts by running them along a narrow trench. When gravel or concrete is tamped in place above these devices, the posts become very hard to uproot.

DRIVEN FENCE POSTS

Where the soil is free of rocks, small-diameter fence posts can often be driven directly into the ground. This simple procedure does away with the bother of digging holes and tamping in fill; however, it seldom produces a fence that is plumb and straight. Some types of rustic stake fences are erected in this manner. The irregularities in the post alignment merely add to the charm of the fence.

To drive wooden posts, you can slip a capped sleeve of heavy pipe over the end of the fence and use it as a driver or you can pound the sleeve with a heavy hammer. The sleeve protects the top of the post from splintering. If the post is stopped short by bed rock, saw off the top at fence height. If you are planning to drive a great many posts, you will find that a portable platform may make it easier for you to swing the maul down on the top of the post. A light platform 2 or 3 feet in height will enable you to get a full swing when you start a 6-foot post.

ATTACHING TOP RAILS

All your painstaking work in lining up the posts will be wasted if your rails are not attached firmly and squarely to the posts. There are several accepted methods of fastening rails to posts, depending on the type of fence under construction and on the durability desired in the fence.

First step, regardless of the method chosen for attaching the rails, is to apply paint or preservative to all surfaces where the rails and posts touch, for protection against decay. If paint is used, brush a generous coating of good quality base paint on both rail and post and attach the two while it is still wet. When the paint dries, it will seal the crevices. If the fence is to be left unpainted, coat the surfaces with a colorless wood preservative (see above).

Lap joints—The simplest and commonest joint used in attaching rails is the lap joint. The rail is merely laid against or on top of the post and nailed in place. Top rails are commonly attached in this manner, even though the bottom rails may be attached by some other method. Rails lapped against

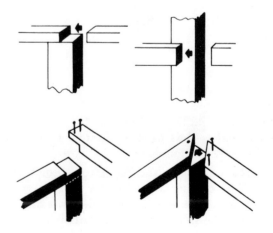

the side of the post are not strong enough to support heavy weight, for most of the strain is carried by the nails. For this reason, rails so attached are usually used only to carry light pickets or are used by themselves, as in a post-and-rail fence.

Butt joints—Another common fence joint is the butt joint. Rails are simply held against the post and toenailed in place. If the rails are wedged

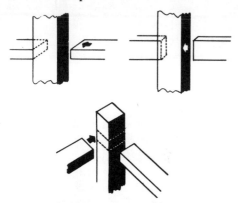

tightly between the posts, this type of joint is stronger than the lap joint because the posts help to support the end of the rail by friction. Rails so attached can be used to support vertical boards, grape stakes, and heavy pickets. This joint is not recommended, however, for louver fencing.

Grooved joint—A more substantial joint is made by cutting a groove or "dado" into the post and fitting

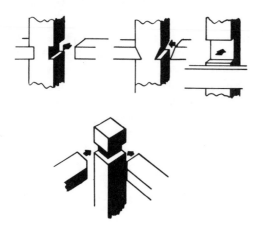

the rail into it. This type of joint is a good weight-bearer and is thus used for bottom rails of louver or heavy board fences.

Mortised joint — Another strong joint can be formed by cutting a rectangular hole (or mortise) partly or all the way through the post and sliding the tip of the rail (tenon) into it. This joint is common in post and rail fencing, although it is frequently found in pre-built picket fences. It is clean, neat, and strong; but it is a difficult one for an amateur to fashion. If you plan to cut mortises in the posts, you will find it easier to work on them if you lay the posts flat on the ground. *Caution:* Make sure

that the bottom rail is level before setting the post permanently in place.

An imitation mortise-and-tenon joint can be easily assembled for a post and rail fence. The post is laminated of three layers of lighter wood, such as

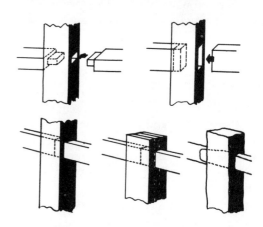

1x4's to produce a 3x4 post, or 2x4's to produce a 6x4 post. The middle layer is omitted where the

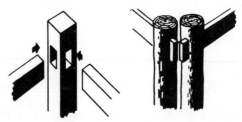

rail passes through the post, thus forming a mortise. Posts of this type are more likely to deteriorate than solid ones, because they are difficult to seal against moisture penetration.

ATTACHING PICKETS AND BOARDS

Once you have finished installing your posts and rails, you will find the rest of the job is easy—but tedious. Attaching pickets is a simple operation, but if you have many to nail on, you will be very relieved to drive home the last nail in the last picket. For instance, in erecting a 100-foot stretch of grape stake fencing, you will drive more nails than you would to attach siding to a 5-room house!

Before you attach the pickets, you should make provision to protect them against decay in the same manner as you treated the rails. They are vulnerable to fungus attack where they are attached to the rails, and should be given a protective coating of paint or preservative. As with the rails, attaching the pickets while the paint is wet will produce a more secure weather seal.

When pickets, slats, or boards are to be attached with an opening between each, here is a simple way to keep the spacing uniform; Cut a slat the exact width of the opening and attach a small cleat to one end. Hang it by the cleat on the rail alongside an attached picket, place the next picket against it, and nail the picket to the rail. Shift the cleat over one, and repeat. See drawing.

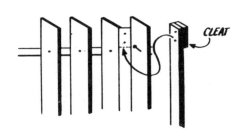

Pickets or boards placed snugly against each other will pull apart in time. If you desire a crackless fence, use tongue-and-groove, sleeved siding, or plywood sheeting.

Pickets should not be allowed to touch the soil. At least 2 inches clearance is advisable.

PAINTING

White is the traditional color for fences. It gives an appearance of neatness, complements floral display, calls attention to the fence in dim light, and sets a positive boundary line. Colored fences are frequently introduced as part of a garden design, to relate the fence to the house, brighten a wooden section of the property, liven up the play yard, or complement the floral color scheme.

For long fence life, and infrequent repainting, use the best quality paints that you can obtain. For a superior finish, apply a base coat, and after it dries, brush on two coats of outdoor paint. You will find the application easier if you paint the pieces before they are assembled, as it is difficult to reach all parts and crevices with the brush after the fence is completed. When the fence is assembled, you can touch up hammer marks, hand prints, and nail heads.

Fences that resemble house siding, or those with large flat surfaces can be painted with an exterior type paint roller. There are rollers designed to paint in V-grooved siding and for corner work, though you may have to touch up a few spots with a brush.

Your paint dealer can recommend the best finish for your particular climate. If you are planning to plant against the fence, watch for mildew deposits; perhaps use a mildewcide in your finish. Remember that some garden sprays will stain painted finishes. Flush the fence with water immediately, if spray gets on the fence.

Caution: If white lead paint is applied to a fence that is penning in stock, the animals should be kept away from it while the paint is wet. Cows are fond of fresh paint and can lick off enough to get lead poisoning.

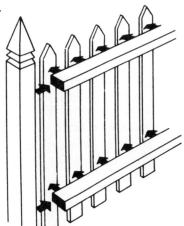

Water-mixed casein paint is an inexpensive and popular substitute for oil-based paint. It is superior to whitewash and, if properly applied and of top quality, it often lasts as long as oil-based paint. Be sure to get the outdoor variety. It is sold boxed in powder form, ready to be mixed with water.

Stains can be applied to a natural fence, but many of them merely color and do not preserve the wood. Ask for a type that contains varnish, creosote, or linseed oil. Special stains have been developed for redwood that preserve its natural color. Stain has to be re-applied more often than paint.

One form of wood preservative, that is naturally green in color, can be used as a stain, if the color is suitable. It will protect the fence against decay but will not shield it from the effects of sunlight. It can be painted over.

Fences in the country are often spray painted, but this method is inadvisable (if not illegal) in the city. Wind can carry the paint droplets some distance and deposit them like permanent dew on neighbors' cars and windows. Furthermore, spray painting often does not give the lasting surface that a skillfully handled brush can provide, and it must therefore be renewed more frequently.

In skilled hands, however, a spray gun can quickly apply paint to fences that would be impossible to paint by hand, such as split rail, chain link, or 10-mile stretches of post and rail. Attachments have been developed that permit both sides of a fence to be sprayed simultaneously.

CARE and REPAIR . . . a springtime chore

Even the best of fences requires some maintenance and repair. Wind, rain, frost, corrosive breezes, wood-boring insects all take their toll.

Spring is a good time to inspect the fence line for damage inflicted during the winter. If the rains have been heavy, the posts may be waterlogged and starting to decay. Examine them at the ground line for signs of rot and dig away the soil to see how they are faring below the surface. If some decay is discernible, chip out the infected wood, and drench with a toxic wood preservative.

Check over alignment of posts and pound down any that have been forced up by heaving of the soil due to frost action or drying of adobe clay. Drive home any nails that have been worked loose by wind pressure on the boards, shifting of the post, or warping of the wood.

If the post has canted out of plumb, force it into line (an automobile jack is handy for tasks of this kind), brace it straight, and tamp the soil down around the base. If the soil seems too unstable to hold the post, increase the base of the post by digging out around it and pouring a concrete collar. If the slant of the posts is due to wind pressure, you may have to brace the fence on the weather side with guy wires or boards, or add small offshoot fences to the lee side that will serve to brace the fence and also add interest to your garden; or, if the fence is a solid-panel type, you may have to replace some of the air-tight panels with openwork to reduce the wind resistance. If your fence continues to lean after you have tried these remedies, you may have to devise some baffles to detour the wind currents away from the structure. When you reach this point, you should probably call for professional help.

Late spring is also a good time to check the plantings and miscellaneous vegetation alongside the fence. If a lush growth of weeds is seeking sanctuary from the hoe along the fence. turn them under or spray them with a toxicant and form a firebreak. Inspect vines and climbing roses growing beside the fence for tendrils that have worked themselves into the fence joints where they will pry it apart. Prune plantings where they rub against galvanized fencing so they will not corrode the zinc plating off the wire.

If paint has started to blister or flake away, brush it clean with a wire brush and repaint. Paint should be applied as often as the house itself needs it.— usually, 3 to 5 years.

REPAIRING ROTTED POSTS

If a post rots away at the ground level, there are three ways of repairing it: it may be replaced with a new one set in place a foot or so away, a new section can be set in alongside the old one and at-

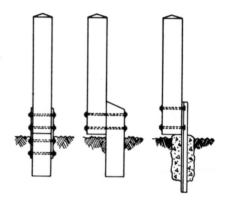

tached to the top of the old one, or the rotted section of the post may be sawed out and steel braces bolted to the top and bottom parts of the original post.

If it is necessary to remove a sound, whole post, you will require mechanical assistance. To extract a post from the soil takes a great deal of leverage. This can be supplied by a post puller that you can

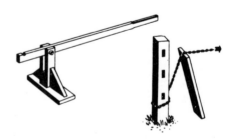

buy in some localities or make yourself, as shown in the drawing. If the post is located where you can reach it with a tractor, you can pull it out with a cable or chain as shown.

FENCE LAWS . . . stay on the safe side

This section is intended to suggest the principal legal problems which the landowner should have in mind in erecting and maintaining fences. It is not exhaustive, nor is it possible to provide answers to those problems in individual cases. Answers will often differ, depending upon the state and locality in which the land is located.

SOURCES OF LAWS AND REGULATIONS COVERING FENCES

State laws, local ordinances, and restrictions contained in deeds and covenants relating to land are the principal sources of laws and restrictions which the landowner should know about and take into account in building fences. These vary from state to state and even from neighborhood to neighborhood, so are too numerous to set out here. They are important, however, particularly in closely settled areas, for failure to observe them may result in a fence that must be torn down and rebuilt on a different set-back line or to conform to required specifications.

The first thing to look at is the deed and title report, to learn whether restrictions have been placed on the land by former owners. If a qualified fencing contractor is employed, he should be familiar with state laws and local ordinances. Neighbors also may be helpful; but, as with new construction of any kind, it is not safe to assume that a new fence is a proper one merely because it is similar to older existing fences in the neighborhood. New zoning ordinances may have been passed after the older fences were built. In cases where doubt exists, it is well to seek competent advice before building.

IS IT EVER A LEGAL REQUIREMENT TO HAVE A FENCE?

Generally a landowner can fence or not as he chooses, but there are some situations where proper fences are legally required, or where failure to fence can lead to serious liability. To cite the most common example, owners of livestock must keep them on their own property (except in open range country) or pay for damages they cause. A landowner in some states also risks liability for injuries to children caused by unusual hazards on his land, which are attractive to children, if he does not take steps to make them reasonably inaccessible. This so-called "attractive nuisance" doctrine is not generally applied to swimming pools and ponds, as long as there is no unusually hazardous feature about them; but in some states (including California) *abandoned excavations* dangerous to children must be fenced or covered under peril of criminal as well as civil penalties.

ADJOINING LANDOWNERS

Additional problems arise when the fence to be built is one between adjoining landowners. Fences are generally considered as belonging to the land on which they are built, and a line- or division-fence belongs to the neighboring property owners as tenants in common. An accurately surveyed boundary is necessary to assure that the fence is being put where it is intended to be.

It is desirable, if possible, to have an agreement with the adjoining owner in advance, determining the location and type of fence and dividing up the responsibility for building and maintaining it. Such agreements, which should be in writing for the sake of definiteness and in order to be binding under the laws of some states, can avoid many distressing disputes later on. They can be recorded in most states with the effect of fixing the responsibility for maintenance between future purchasers of the property.

Line fences erected by adjoining landowners together are usually placed on the property line, partly on the property of each, and are commonly owned. However, it is not always possible to secure the concurrence and aid of a neighbor in erecting a fence and in such cases it is advisable to place the fence entirely on the land of the builder, or an inch or so inside the line to allow for possible errors in the survey. Such a fence is wholly the property of the landowner and he need not consult with his neighbor regarding its erection or maintenance as long as it does not violate any law, ordinance, or restrictive covenant.

Most states have laws to the effect that coterminous owners of "improved" or "enclosed" property are jointly obligated even without an agreement to bear the cost of erecting and maintaining line fences. If an adjoining owner chooses to let his land lie "unimproved" or "unenclosed" (depending upon the language of the particular statute), he need not contribute, but if he afterwards improves or encloses his land, he becomes obligated under the laws of some states to pay half the value of fences built by his neighbors and assumes a share of subsequent maintenance costs. These laws are not uniform from state to state, and competent advice may be required to determine whether a legally enforcible obligation exists in particular instances. However, a landowner who improves his land after neighbors have fenced one or more sides will usually find it to his benefit to acquire an interest in these fences in order to have a voice in the manner in which they are maintained and in order to decorate his side as he chooses.

Division fences provide many opportunities for disputes. The solution of such disputes by force of law is not always satisfactory because neighbors must go on living next to each other afterwards. A reasonable amount of cooperation in the erection and maintenance of fences for the mutual satisfaction of all can avoid or settle most of the problems.

LOS ANGELES POOL FENCING LAW

In June of 1956 the City of Los Angeles adopted an ordinance which requires homeowners to provide certain safeguards around private swimming pools. In view of the increasing number of private pools, it is to be expected that other municipalities will follow suit with similar ordinances. Since existing laws often serve as guideposts for new legislation, pool owners might profit by studying the Los Angeles requirements before building any new fence which might not conform to a future code in their area.

Specifically, the Los Angeles ordinance states that the pool owner must provide a 4½-foot fence or a competent person who shall keep the pool under observation at all times while water is kept in the pool, or a pool cover or other protective device approved by the Board of Building and Safety Commissioners.

A further clause states that the Board may make slight modifications with respect to the fence height or to the nature or the position of any gate latch, and may permit other protective devices equal to the protection offered by the required fence and gate.

Other new amendments to an older established ordinance prohibit building any pool over 18 inches deep where fences required for purposes of safety conflict with existing fence and yard restrictions.

The purpose of the ordinance is to make it impossible for small children to gain access to the pool. You can fence the perimeter of your property, or in the immediate pool area as long as the fence keeps out youngsters. You don't have to fence if you can prove that the pool is permanently supervised, or protected by an approved pool cover when no lifeguard is on duty.